Bringing the Outdoors In

Bringing the

Outdoors In

HOW TO DO WONDERS WITH
VINES, WILDFLOWERS, FERNS, MOSSES,
BULBS, CACTI, AND DOZENS OF OTHER
PLANTS MOST PEOPLE OVERLOOK

written and illustrated by
Peter Loewer

CONTEMPORARY
BOOKS

CHICAGO · NEW YORK

Published by Contemporary Books, Inc.
180 North Michigan Avenue, Chicago, Illinois 60601

Published simultaneously in Canada by Beaverbooks, Ltd.
195 Allstate Parkway, Valleywood Business Park
Markham, Ontario L3R 4T8 Canada

ISBN: 0-8092-4574-4

Library of Congress Catalog Card Number: 73-83863

Printed in the United States of America.

First published in the United States of America in
1974 by the Walker Publishing Company, Inc.

Contents

List of Plants Illustrated

Preface

When my wife and I decided to leave the hectic glamour of city life and return to rural green, my house-plant collection was bequeathed to friends and acquaintances. We had rented a van for furniture and books that in no way resembled the effortless moving commercials seen on TV; our car was stacked to the roof with my wife, her mother, the best china, two Siamese cats struggling to escape from pet carriers, enough food for a week, boxes of art supplies, and an unabridged dictionary, all of which left no earthly room for plants. Besides, I rationalized, our future home was surrounded by fields, wild flowers, and trees, providing ample evidence of nature.

We moved in July, had the rudiments of plumbing by August, a chaotic kitchen by September, and our first nature walk in October. We worked on the house all winter, occasionally peeking through frost-covered windows at acres of awesome white, and by the following March were literally bonkers. After ten years of the relative camouflage provided by city brick and steel, we had forgotten the majesty of a northern winter.

The following spring, I had the choice of installing new gutters or building a small window greenhouse. Naturally, I chose the latter. The roof could make do another year, but obviously we couldn't.

The next hurdle was filling the window with greenery. I didn't know then about buying plants by mail, and the nearest commercial suppliers were miles away. In a short time, neighbors brought cuttings and plants from their collections, including many that had been in the family for generations. In the fall, I brought in some annuals from our pathetic attempt at a formal country garden, and looked about the woods and fields for other likely subjects. By November, the window greenhouse was filled and helped us to get through the worst winter we have experienced to date.

That was four years ago. We still haven't finished the house (some say we never will, as remodeling is a lifetime occupation). But the spring beauty bloomed this morning—a bleak and gray day in early March—tiny pink blossoms that grace the spring woods were curled over the edge of a clay pot in the window greenhouse. Spring cyclamen, tulips, hyacinths, daffodils, azaleas and freesias have brightened the sun porch since late December. By the end of the afternoon, the foamflower buds will push their way through the soil and the lily will bloom for Easter. Two white cattleya orchids command the center of the dining-room table, surrounded by a spray of "dancing doll" orchids, spots of bright yellow and brown that move in the breeze of passing-by. The Christmas poinsettia still holds its scarlet bracts, though its tiny flowers have fallen off. Next week, the columnea will be a six-foot mass of red, and then the cactus will dot the windowsills with white, pink, and yellow.

In a world that daily flirts with disaster, continually teetering on the brink of hysteria, where the unbelievable has become the commonplace, and crises upon crises are flung at you from newspaper and TV, it's very easy to lose your orientation and find yourself asking where the time has gone. But when you think of the last time you saw a violet in spring, an apple tree weighted with blossoms, or the annual display of an African amaryllis, once again you can sense the true passage of time.

This book is the result of working with plants over four long winters in an effort to recapture the meaning of time.

Introduction

Each chapter in this book deals with a specific subject relating to growing plants or groups of plants.

Chapter 1 looks at plant growth, reproduction, and structure of plants. It is my firm belief an informed thumb is a green thumb. We all know that plants need light to exist, but when you realize the complexities involved, and when you remember that you have the responsibility for a living thing, it's somehow easier to make the effort in moving a plant that needs more light rather than putting it off with the idea that you'll get around to it later.

Chapter 2 shows how to construct small indoor greenhouses using existing windows without a large outlay of money or time. The average home carpenter should be at ease with the specifications, and I've tried to list all the materials needed.

Chapter 3 lists standard potting mixes and also defines a number of commercially available soil components to help the grower in devising his own. The pH reading is at best a debatable point with many people (some never pay it a second thought) and many plants will struggle along in just about any kind of medium that will hold their roots, but these will never reward you with their best efforts. In the wrong soil, the majority of wild flowers and bog plants won't even struggle, they'll just fade away. Soil-less plant mixes are a fairly new arrival on the horticultural scene. I have never been overly involved with them because we have an active compost heap in the back yard and a ready source of leaf mold from the woods, but many people live in suburbs and cities, where soil is not easy to obtain, especially in large amounts, so I've included recipes for these mixes.

Chapter 4 deals with pots and the variety that is available today, along with information on the new self-watering pots.

Chapter 5 concerns the different methods of plant propagation. It's not meant to be a definitive treatise, but shows the many techniques used.

Chapter 6 describes how to set up a terrarium, and how to stock it with some interesting plants found in nature. Once again, it does not list every native plant that would work in a bottle garden, but common representative types of each. It is assumed that any plant hobbyist who is more than casually interested will check the bibliography in pursuit of more information.

Chapters 7 thru 11 deal with varieties of plants that grow in unique and individual manners, and suggests equipment that will help these plants on their way.

Chapter 12 concerns insectivorous plants, how to care for them, and where to look for natural specimens. If a field trip into swamp is not exactly your idea of a great afternoon, then consult Chapter 16 for commercial sources of supply.

Chapter 13 gives an easy method for forcing outdoor bulbs for winter bloom. Once again, it does not list every bulb that is capable of flowering with this treatment, only those that I've grown.

Chapter 14 is a compendium of garden plants that may be brought indoors, gift plants exchanged on holidays and kept all year instead of being tossed out when the blooms have faded, flowering plants that may be easily grown from seed to bloom indoors, and a couple of time-honored house plants that tend to be overlooked because they are thought to be old-hat.

Chapter 15 lists the more common ailments that will afflict plants in the home. While not a strict organic cultist, I do have a healthy suspicion of many of the chemicals that are freely sold today, know that they do the job, but having read labels, prefer to leave them to the expert, and rely on more mundane methods.

Chapter 16 lists sources of supply, magazines, and plant societies.

The Appendix gives some informational tables, and the bibliography lists a great many books, available for sale or in libraries, for the person who would like to delve a bit deeper into any aspect of this book.

I have tried to avoid endless listings of plants that can be grown indoors. Not only would that be a bore to read, but such lists have been published by the score. Instead, I've chosen a smaller number of plants, grown them in average home conditions and prepared the drawings from live plants, in the belief that photographs in books rarely succeed in describing the living feel of a plant, unless priced out of the reach of the average buyer and presented in a coffee-table format.

Undoubtedly, I have also made mistakes. One of my favorite plants could possibly be twice as large and three times as beautiful if I had known a different approach, but I'll never know until someone else points it out, and as yet, I've never been disappointed in any of them.

In addition to family, I wish to extend heartfelt thanks to the following people for their help in preparation of this book: Mrs. C. F. Rogers of Hialeah for introducing me to the plant life of Florida; Mr. Douglas Heinle of Cochecton Center, New York, for donning his Post Office hat with efficiency and dignity thereby proving that the United States Postal Service can work; Mr. Richard K. Winslow, my editor, for his encouragement of and patience with this project; Ms. Barbara Huntley, art director of Walker, for her welcome assistance and unerring sense of design; and lastly Mr. T. Williard DeSantis of Narrowsburg, New York, for his inventive mind, creative approach to carpentry, and invaluable aid in developing the plans for construction.

CHAPTER ONE
The Plant World

A plant is a living thing. It's subject to the same rules and regulations that govern the human body. Without light, plants become anemic; without air, water, and food, they slowly waste away. Too much heat or too much cold will generally do them in. Without an occasional rest, they push themselves to an early demise, and without routine maintenance, they quickly appear unshaven and unshorn. Like people, plants respond to extra attention, although I'm not fully convinced that a carrot screams when yanked from the earth or a philodendron reacts to my innermost fears.

In order to get the best results from your house plants, it is important to understand something of the mechanisms that are basic to their growth and development. It's much easier to pinch back a favorite plant if you know why such a process works, and that the pinching will not harm it in any way.

I freely admit that no one seeing a newly bloomed cattleya orchid, cries out: "Did you ever see such a beautiful inflorescence?" Or upon spying an emergent white fly calls: "There's an Aleyrodidae on the pinnately compound leaf of my *Calamus ciliaris!*" Perhaps a turn-of-the-century, die-hard botanist in an Elinor Glyn novel would utter such a mouthful, but not the typical horticulturist of today.

However, when you have trouble with your plants, or when you are particularly proud of a specimen that you've slaved over and you want it to keep its spectacular health, it really helps to have a basic working knowledge of plants and their nomenclature under your belt. Once you become seriously interested in growing plants, you will find that basic reference works like Graf's *Exotic Plant Manual* and the many horticultural magazines require a good basic botanical vocabulary.

TYPICAL PLANT CELL

All living things, whether plant or animal, are made up of individual units called cells. Usually, these cells are too small to be seen without a lens or a microscope. Some bacteria, the smallest examples of plant life, consist of a single cell, 1/50,000 of an inch in diameter. The giant sequoias of California are over 350 feet tall and consist of countless trillions of cells. Not that you're about to grow a mature sequoia in your living room, but when you care for a smaller plant you are not only the guardian of leaves, stems, and roots, but you take responsibility for all the cells that make up the plant—each one needing water, air, and food.

To form a three-dimensional picture of a typical plant cell, let's imagine a plastic Baggie about the size required for an average tuna-fish sandwich. Now we add the following ingredients:

1 thirty green peas to represent *chloroplasts*, the food-manufacturing units of plant cells. Chloroplasts contain *chlorophyll* (of chewing gum fame) and give plants their green color; they are responsible for the process of photosynthesis.

2 a handful of sand, each grain representing a *ribosome.* These organelles (literally, a small organ) aid in the production of protein, enabling many plants to become meat substitutes in most of the world.

3 three tablespoons of dried lentils which will become *mitochondria*, organelles that assist the plant cell in the chemical activities relating to respiration.

4 a few tablespoons of tapioca, representing *leucoplasts*, the organelles of starch formation. Any excess carbohydrates produced by a plant

5 one marshmallow stuffed with a few kidney beans and three or four yards of sewing thread. The marshmallow is a stand-in for the *nucleus* or "brain" and controls all the activities of the other organelles and structures, since it determines when the cell is to grow, to divide, and to die. The kidney beans become *nucleoli*, rich in protein and helpmates in the process of cell division. The thread acts as the *chromosomes*, genetic components of every living cell and dictators of the cell's heredity.

Now fill the remainder of the bag with plain water and seal the top. The water represents *cytoplasm*, the basic liquid of a cell that holds all the organelles and structures in suspension. When the cell nucleus is included in any discussion of a cell, the cytoplasm is termed *protoplasm*.

We now have a very soft and malleable model of a plant cell, about ten thousand times larger than its real-life counterpart.

But plant cells are not soft, and here we have a major distinction between plants and animals: the structure of the cell wall. In animals, cell walls are like our Baggie until bones, skin, shells and other tough materials hold them in shape. Plants rely on a thicker cell wall that contains cellulose and can easily be pictured by putting our cell model into a slightly larger cardboard box, much like the containers used to freeze vegetables.

The following diagram shows a typical plant cell as seen under an electron microscope, (1) nucleus, (2) nucleoli (3) chromosomes, (4) leucoplasts, (5) ribosomes, (6) mitochondria, (7) chloroplasts, (8) cytoplasm, (9) cell wall.

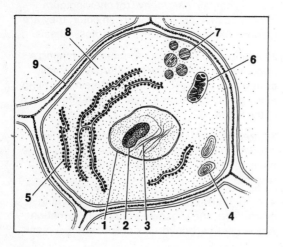

In addition to cell walls, the more advanced plants (like the trees and flowering plants) have specialized cells to act as supports and conduct water throughout their systems. Plants like the mosses and molds lack these additional supports and can never grow any larger than they are at present.

THE LIFE PROCESSES OF A PLANT CELL

Most plants have the ability to transform simple substances into their food. The most important of these substances, taken from the soil and atmosphere, are carbon dioxide and water. In combination with chlorophyll (manufactured in the chloroplasts), when triggered by sunlight or artificial light, carbon dioxide and water combine to produce carbohydrates in the form of dextrose, the staple form of energy for a plant. At the same time, pure oxygen is produced as a by-product. This process is called *photosynthesis*. The chemical process is really simple. Water contains hydrogen and oxygen. Carbon dioxide consists of carbon and oxygen. In the presence of radiant energy, chlorophyll produces dextrose, which is a chemical combination of carbon, hydrogen, and oxygen with excess oxygen released into the surrounding air. Those plants we associate with dark, dank, and gloomy places, such as molds, mildews, and mushrooms, do not have chlorophyll and are unable to photosynthesize their own food. Instead, they live on the remains of other plants and animals. Or, thriving in our kitchens, they exist on stale pieces of bread.

Photosynthesis is, without doubt, the single most important chemical process in the world. Directly or indirectly, all of our food comes from plants. Just as vital, the oxygen that all living things require to convert food into energy is a direct result of photosynthesis. The green plant is the *only* significant source of free oxygen in our atmosphere. I cringe at the sight of rich farmland, ripped up and coated with layers of blacktop—for here is dead land.

In most plants (exceptions are the cacti and other succulents) the leaf is the center of the photosynthetic process. The exchanges of oxygen, carbon dioxide, and water vapor occur in small openings on the undersurface of the leaf. These openings, called *stomata*, are easily visible under a hand lens as minute pores. At 300X they look like this:

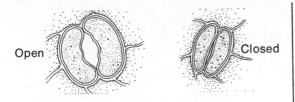

Open

Closed

During the day, water pressure builds up within the stomata walls, forcing them open. At night they lose water, collapse inward, becoming more or less closed. Water is lost through these pores as water vapor, to be replaced by water drawn up from the roots. This process is called transpiration and, even in the advanced botanical sciences of today, is not fully understood. It's assumed that since the stomata must be open during the day to take in air, the loss of water is a side effect, beyond the plant's control.

One of the major problems that plants have in today's well-heated homes (most plants welcomed the Energy Crisis with open leaves!) is in maintaining a balance between the water lost from the stomata and the overly dry conditions surrounding them. Remember, the humidity in an average heated home is about 15 percent. Even the vast sandy and parched Sahara Desert enjoys an annual average of 25 percent humidity, so you can see why house plants, especially tropicals, appreciate a frequent application of water with a misting can or atomizer.

Of the four major methods of home heating (hot-air, hot-water, steam, and electric) the last is one of the best for plants because the heat is relatively constant—there is no fan or forced air equipment needed to move the heat around. Hot-water heating is the next best; the changes in temperature are always gradual. Hot-air heating has a definite drying effect, especially if a plant is placed in front of a heating duct; the steady blast of hot air dries out the leaves quickly, and the roots need additional waterings as the soil becomes rapidly depleted of water. By liberal placement of gravel and pans filled with water, the humidity can be re-established. Or you might consider adding a humidifier to the furnace system. It's a relatively inexpensive addition, and the additional humidity benefits plants, furniture, and people. Steam heat causes rapid fluctuations in temperature, and plants must be kept away from pipes. (When any of the plants described in later chapters have particular temperature needs, I'll cite them individually.)

Since the stomata close at night, you will occasionally find drops of water at the tips of the leaves in the morning, especially those of the tropicals. Don't worry about it. When the stomata are closed, roots continue to absorb water, and any excess is released in droplets through special pores in the leaf tips. This occurs so that the plant maintains an even water pressure within. It's called *guttation* and sounds a great deal worse than it is.

THREE KEYS TO HEALTHY PLANTS

For your plants to flourish, you must see that they photosynthesize efficiently. This means they must get the proper amount of light, air, and water.

Light

Light intensity is measured in foot candles (FC). One FC is the amount of light cast on a white surface by one candle, one foot way, in an otherwise dark room. You can measure FC's with a photo exposure meter, using the simple FC conversion tables found in the camera instruction manual. If you've lost the manual, as I have, you will find a table in the Appendix that will convert meter readings to FC.

Plants that need full sun, such as cacti and most flowering annuals, generally require about 6000 to 8000 FC. Plants such as ferns and most begonias prefer partial shade or an average of 2000 FC, and plants like the deep jungle dwellers, require full shade or between 100 and 500 FC. Many plants will survive in 20 FC of light but 100 FC seems to be the minimum for growth.

Windows immediately cut down on light intensity with the loss of light through outside refraction of the glass and the fact that some light is actually absorbed by the glass. Now add architectural details such as eaves and cornices and more light is lost. A west window in mid-morning may read 400 FC at the inside sill, but only 10 FC six feet into the room, while the outside reading is over 10,000 FC. If windows are lightly curtained, screened, or dirty (a major problem of the city dweller) more light is lost. Now add a layer of dust to the leaf tops and the amount of light received by the leaves is dim indeed. Plants should be dusted right along with books, table tops, and everything else. Remember a comfortable light for reading is 50 FC, but it's hardly enough to keep a plant alive, much less healthy.

In all the plant descriptions, I've included the light requirements in terms of Full Sun, Partial Shade, and Shady. The Foot Candle routine is your necessary first step to find the areas in your home that produce the optimum light needed.

Plants Under Lights

A new world has opened up for the plant lover who is denied adequate natural light for good plant growth. This is the method of growing plants under artificial light, using a combination of fluorescent and tungsten lighting. The process is a whole volume in itself, and the bibliography lists two excellent books available on the subject. All the plants in this book may be grown under lights, even in a closet, if the light intensities are high enough.

Carbon Dioxide

Because carbon dioxide contains both carbon and oxygen in the only source readily available to a plant, it's of primary importance to the process of photosynthesis and healthy plant growth. I've always thought that the success of many "green-thumbers" might be due to not only the constant attention they give to their plants but the breathing they do in the plant area, giving the plants an extra shot of carbon dioxide with every breath. The plants literally grow on every word. I don't advocate hyperventilating for your plants every morning but there just might be something to it.

Generally enough carbon dioxide is available in the surrounding air to provide for a plant's needs, but there are many experiments in horticulture today which are trying to increase plant growth by releasing measured amounts of this gas in greenhouse atmospheres. The results in increased growth rate can be startling. The more sophisticated garden and plant catalogs sell automatic equipment for this purpose.

Water

Although water is needed by the plant to bring minerals from the earth and provide the basic ingredient for cytoplasm and the hydrogen for the photosynthetic process, the side effects of wilting can be disastrous. When a leaf wilts, the stomata close to prevent further water loss. Naturally this cuts down on the intake of carbon dioxide. As a result, the plant cannot use the carbon and oxygen to produce the dextrose needed for energy on the cellular level, and must rely on its reserves. If a plant has not wilted too badly, it will generally snap back, but successive wiltings damage it both with respect to cell damage and loss of potential food energy.

RESPIRATION AROUND THE CLOCK

Respiration is the process that supplies cells with the oxygen they need to convert the food produced by photosynthesis into energy. All plant and animal cells respire. Breathing is a purely mechanical activity developed by many animals in which large amounts of oxygen are allowed to reach the cells deep inside the body. Most animals need this additional oxygen to provide the energy required for movement. A plant does not breathe as animals do, but absorbs the needed oxygen through the roots, stems and stomata. In essence, all plants and animals respire, but only animals breathe.

Respiration occurs twenty-four hours a day in every living plant cell. Each cell absorbs the needed oxygen through the stomata, and also by diffusion through the roots and stems, releasing carbon dioxide as a waste product. Photosynthesis occurs during daylight hours, only in

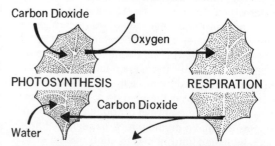

Carbon Dioxide

Oxygen

PHOTOSYNTHESIS   RESPIRATION

Carbon Dioxide

Water

those cells that have chloroplasts and generally in the plant leaves, taking in carbon dioxide and the hydrogen from water, producing food and releasing oxygen as a by-product. If the two processes proceeded at an equal rate, with respiration using the oxygen and food as quickly as photosynthesis produced it, there would be no left-overs for growth and repair. Fortunately, photosynthesis occurs at a faster rate and a surplus of food and oxygen is produced. Thus a plant in a sealed container, given an initially adequate supply of water and soil, and ample light, may exist for years without outside help. This is the reason that a sealed terrarium works.

Temperature plays an important part in plant respiration. As temperatures fall, the activities of respiration decrease. Generally a ten-degree drop is considered the best. That is, a ten-degree drop from the average daytime temperature that a particular plant enjoys. If your plant does best in 70° during the day, try to give it 60° at night; if it likes 60° during the day, give it 50° at night. Most plant growth occurs at night. That ten-degree drop gives the plant additional aid in the digestion of the sugars it has produced during the day.

Once we know about the effect of temperature, we can prolong the life of a favorite flower on a plant. Blossoms on azaleas, orchids, lilies, tulips, and the rest will last longer if given a cool night. Like leaves, flowers are made of individual cells that continue to respire and grow, even if cut, and dropping the temperature slows everything down. When we go on vacation, I always move the plants to a cooler part of the house to slow down their activity. This also cuts down on their water intake and hopefully they won't dry out in our absence.

Not too long ago, people were so worried about the respiration activities of plants and flowers, they removed them from bedrooms and hospital rooms at night. They believed the carbon dioxide levels would become so high that human life would be in danger of suffocation. Experiments have shown that a greenhouse in early morning produces an increase of only one half of one percent carbon dioxide, but a crowded room at a cocktail party can raise the concentration fully one percent!

DORMANCY

Everything in life must rest at one time or another, and plants are no exception. After they have finished flowering and the leaves have manufactured adequate food for the next year, plants usually enter a period of dormancy. This "quiet time" in a plant's life is governed by the natural cycle of growth and a combination of shorter days and a drop in temperature. Dormancy is particularly noticeable with plants from the temperate regions of the world. Tropicals are not so obvious, as they hold their leaves throughout the year, but few plants will flower, fruit, and continue to bear new leaves on a year-round basis. If they are forced to overwork for long periods of time, plants will ultimately die, literally worn out from overwork.

Most of the plants brought in from out-of-doors will slow down their growth for the bleaker part of the winter. Many of our wild flowers and spring bulbs will not produce flowers at all, if not given a period of rest in combination with cooler temperatures.

Trees give ample evidence of dormancy by dropping their leaves in autumn. Small northern trees are occasionally used for bonsai subjects. Every autumn their leaves turn color and fall, even though they are indoors, but your passion flower, growing by the window, will keep its green and leafy look all winter long. It will not flower or produce new leaves and will continue to rest until the coming spring. When plants are dormant, watering should be held to a minimum, just enough to keep the plant from shriveling up. Fertilizing should be stopped entirely.

LANGUAGE OF PLANTS

Whether talking to your florist or reading horticultural books and journals, it's a big advantage to have a basic botanical vocabulary. If plant instructions say: "Pinch the terminal bud," it's a good idea to know where it is.

The first thing to remember is that all plants known to man have been given their own Latin names. In the 1700's when the present system of classification began, Latin was the international language of scholars, so it was the obvious language to use. Since then it's become a relatively "dead" language, but that's all to the good since unspoken languages do not change. When you think of the many local names for plants that are different from place to place and country to country and generation to generation, it's obvious that some system of identification had to be established so that clear communication could exist between a New Jersey horticulturist and a Japanese botanist, and more important between you and your mail-order nurseryman.

The three terms in general use are: genus, species, and variety. In print, the genus and species are always italicized and the genus has an initial capital letter. The variety has initial capitals, is in Roman type and set off by single quotes. Thus the grape hyacinth found in many modern gardens and window sills is also known as *Muscari armeniacum* 'Heavenly Blue'. The term *Muscari* spp. refers to all the species of the genus *Muscari*.

Not all plants have varietal names, but occasionally a "sport" or mutation will occur, by accident or design, that has a color, leaf shape, or other characteristic that is different from the parent plant. When this characteristic shows up in succeeding generations it is said to "breed true." The new form is not different enough to win its own species name so it is tagged a variety. Occasionally you will see three names in Latin as *Dracaena fragrans* var. *massangeana* (the cornstalk plant of house-plant fame). The third name is still the variety but has been latinized, as the plant was named before the modern code was established, and in keeping with the code, the word "variety" is abbreviated and set in Roman type. You will also run across the same name without the addition of the "var."

In plant breeding, when two species are crossed in a search for new varieties, the resultant plant is called a hybrid. Hybrids do not usually breed true but are propagated by asexual means such as rooted cuttings. Hybrids are signified by naming the parent plants with an x or multiplication sign between the names as: *Euphorbia bupleurifolia* x *clava.* (This plant is a thornless crown of thorns.)

In addition, you'll run across the word "cultivar." This signifies a variety of plant which is known only in cultivation and may or may not be reproduced from seed.

Now why bother? Suppose you wrote to a nursery and ordered a Christmas cactus. The clerk who received your order has a migraine and misreads "cactus" for "candle." A week or more later, depending on the post office, you receive a strange-looking plant, the likes of which you've never imagined could exist, a Christmas candle. If you had ordered a *Schlumbergera bridgesii* you would not have gotten a *Tillandsia imperialis*. Most suppliers now insist on dealing in Latin nomenclature. The majority of these firms print catalogs which describe their products, rather than illustrating them, another reason to familiarize yourself with the accurate terminology.

PLANT TERMINOLOGY

In one of my reference books (Britton and Brown, *Illustrated Flora of the United States and Canada*) there are approximately 600 definitions of words relating to the study of the forms of plants. It is hardly necessary to commit all this terminology to memory but a few definitions are important, just to help in verbal descriptions when tracking down an unknown plant. All of the following terms generally refer to the most advanced members of the plant kingdom, the flowering plants.

Plants that live only one growing season—roots, stems and all—are called *annuals.* Their one function, in a strict biological sense, is to mature so as to flower and cast out seeds. The whole process takes but one season. Many annuals, when given proper conditions, will flower within six weeks from planting the seed. Sweet peas, soybeans, snapdragons, and *Schizanthus pinnatus* (poor man's orchid) are all annuals. Never bemoan the loss of an annual but simply plant more.

Plants that live for two growing seasons are called *biennials.* They generally send up stems and leaves the first year and put out flowers the second. In essence they are annuals that require more time to flower. Beets, carrots, and parsley are all biennials, but they are harvested for food the first year and the flowers are rarely seen.

Perennials are plants that live season after season, either aboveground, such as philodendrons and azaleas, or belowground such as all the bulbs, corms, and tubers. When growing a perennial from seed, do not be disappointed when flowers do not appear the first year. Generally they must grow for a season before flowering. Most house plants are perennials, and remain with us for many years. Occasionally they outlive us; one of my neighbors has a Christmas cactus that goes back to the early 1900's. It occupies a hanging washtub in a basement corner, and since the introduction of hot-air heating in their farmhouse, it is brought upstairs every year in March, a veritable mass of scarlet-pink. Then it blooms for weeks, and finally is banished to the cellar for another year. At this time, it shows no sign of giving up.

Plants with soft stems, such as dandelions, lilies, and morning glories are called *herbs* or *herbaceous plants.* These are not to be confused with the herbs which are grown for flavoring and cooking purposes. Garden parsley, which grows quite well in a small pot for seasoning the year round, is an herb in culinary usage, an herb in botanical usage, and a biennial to boot.

Trees and shrubs that live many years and which grow larger in girth are called *woody* plants.

The difference between herbaceous and woody plants is more distinct in the temperate zone, as many perennials are grown for one season, then killed by cold weather. But when most herbaceous plants are brought indoors and grown year round their once-smooth stems become quite thick and calloused and develop woody tissue. I have an impatiens plant that has been growing now for four years and looks like a miniature tree at the base. The castor bean is another example of a northern annual that becomes a sizable perennial when grown indoors.

A typical flowering plant has the following need-to-know parts:

The terminal bud:

The flowers:

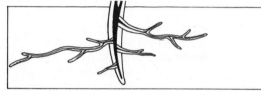

The leaves with the lateral buds between the leaf and stem:

The roots, primary root (vertical) and the lateral roots:

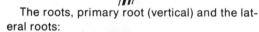

The whole plant aboveground is called the shoot.

When told to pinch back a plant to promote bushy growth, it is the terminal bud that is nipped off. If the plant has more than one stem, each terminal bud may be removed and thus more lateral buds are forced to develop, each of them turning into a stem with leaves and its own terminal bud. Plant hormones are involved in this very intricate and not completely understood process. Many botanists believe that until it is removed the terminal bud puts out a hormone that prevents the lateral buds from developing. It's a kind of safety factor that plants have evolved to give them more than one chance of survival in case of accidents or disease.

Since a complete plant is the total of many intricate parts, let's examine each of the parts and the role it plays to guarantee a healthy plant.

Roots

When a young seedling is beginning to grow it has only one root. As this root grows downward into the soil it produces branches to the side. If one primary root continues to grow alone, and remains the chief root system of the plant, it's called a *tap root*. If the lateral branches soon outstrip the primary root and eventually a mass of roots is formed, the plant has *fibrous roots*. Most of the plants grown for decorative purposes have fibrous roots, and it's a good thing. With so many, a few can be damaged through misadventure without any real harm to the plant.

In addition to the roots growing beneath the ground, there are *aerial roots* and *prop roots* that are found on many house plants. Aerial roots are chiefly found on the tropicals such as philodendrons. Since many tropicals grow in dense jungles, their ground roots are very slight, serving to nourish the plant as it starts its growth upward to the light. Along the way, aerial roots develop to increase the moisture and food available to the plant in addition to acting as supports. When they grow on your philodendrons, leave them alone and congratulate yourself for having given your plant a happy environment. The fiery reed orchid (*Epidendrum ibaguense*) that I recommend later, eventually covers its stems with aerial roots that shoot out in every direction. If you examine these roots closely, you'll see green tips: this is chlorophyll that assists the plant in manufacturing food.

Prop roots are found on many succulents and lend an additional measure of support to the stems. They add an interesting dimension to the stem and look like this:

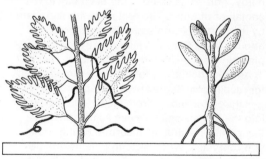

Another word that you will read on occasion is *adventitious*—this refers to a root that occurs in an unusual place or at an unusual time of the plant's development. When leaf cuttings from plants such as coleus and geranium produce roots, these roots are adventitious.

When roots grow in soil or soil mixtures, they form many small root hairs near the tip. These hairs are responsible for the major portion of water that a root system absorbs. They are so

tiny and completely enmeshed in the soil particles, that when transplanted, many hairs are ripped from the parent root. Until the transplanted roots grow new hairs, the plant loses most of its water supply and wilts. Luckily, root hairs grow quickly and the plant usually recovers. After transplanting, it's a good idea to spray additional water on the leaves and cover the plant for a few days with a piece of plastic wrap to serve as a miniature high-humidity greenhouse.

The shock of transplanting is also minimized by moving as much of the original soil that surrounds the root as possible. The older the plant, the safer transplanting becomes.

Many gardeners have grown cuttings or plants in water, and lost them when transplanting them to pots with dirt. If roots are grown in water, they generally do not form root hairs. They have adapted themselves to absorbing the needed oxygen directly from the water. When put into dirt with their small root systems and without the hairs, they tend to dry out before they can grow root hairs. There is a simple remedy. Add some soil or sand each day to the container of water. The root ends are stimulated by the particles, and soon hairs will grow. In about a week they should be ready for transplanting from their sludgy container to real soil.

As I mentioned earlier, all cells need oxygen for respiration. Roots are no exception. The oxygen they need moves from the air aboveground into the tiny spaces between soil particles. At this point, it is directly absorbed by the roots and root hairs. When watering plants, the descending water pulls oxygen in behind it. If the particles are packed too tightly, as in heavy clay soils, there is no room for oxygen and the roots quickly die. A few house plants, like mother-in-law-tongue and the cast iron plant can exist in clay, but they are rare exceptions to the rule. To help, coarse sand or gravel is added to the

basic soil mixes. These hard particles will not meld together, and have air pockets for the oxygen.

What about plants that are purportedly to be watered from below—like African violets? I don't know of any plant, if watered correctly to suit its needs, that should be watered from below unless the soil becomes too dry and shrinks away from the edge of the pot. This happens occasionally to the most dedicated grower; you will know when it happens to you because the water appears in the saucer below as fast as you pour it in from above. Now is the moment for bottom watering. Set the pot in a pan full of water or in the sink and give it a good soak for a couple of hours. The water will rise through the soil by capillary action and completely wet it. Now resume watering from the top as needed. Bottom watering can be quite a chore—imagine doing it to fifty plants! Besides, with the new self-watering pots, water wicks and the like, watering is not the job it used to be.

African violets, by the by, have leaves that spot easily when spattered with water, especially when it's cold. Many growers insist on bottom watering to prevent spotted leaves. Just use warm water and apply it carefully from the top, and you'll have no problems.

Overwatering can rob roots of oxygen too. The soil becomes so saturated, that once again air pockets cannot form and the roots haven't the time to adapt to the process of taking oxygen from water directly. They generally rot before the transformation can occur.

Stems

The stem has several jobs: to support the plant, to bear the leaves, branches, and flowers, to conduct water and minerals to the leaves, and to carry manufactured food to the roots. In the process of evolution, for the plant to survive in changing environments, stems have developed many interesting modifications: they have evolved into bulbs—like the lily—to lead an underground existence; some have become the long trailing *lianas* (a term for a woody climber, generally from the jungle) that hang from trees and carried Tarzan over the gaping maws of the carniverous plants of fiction; they've developed *holdfasts* for ivies and creepers to cling to walls of stone; and some have developed a twisting growth such as the one which carries the morning glory along a slender string. Branches are secondary stems and are called *runners* when they creep along the ground like strawberry runners, and *stolons* when they actively grow below the ground like the lily-of-the-valley or the wild morning glory. Most grassy weeds are well equipped with stolons and it becomes an almost impossible job to prevent their spreading.

Cacti have turned the stem into a self-contained fortress. Their stems provide structural support and also contain chloroplasts, which have replaced the leaves in the manufacture of food. The leaves have evolved into spines, for the defense of the plant.

The *pseudobulbs* of many orchids are modified stems, enabling them to store water for long periods of time.

I've always wondered why many garden books lump corms, tubers, and rhizomes in with bulbs. If they are the same as bulbs, why do they have a different name? Well, they are not the same, but each is a different type of stem with the ability to store food. When you force a bulb, you are really forcing a stem.

Rhizomes are perennial stems that are short and thick and give rise to aboveground branches. Iris, violets, and orchids grow from rhizomes.

Tubers are modified stolons or underground stems swollen with stored food. The sweet potato, potato, and tuberous begonia are tubers.

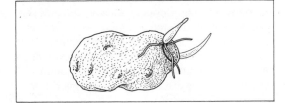

Corms are a series of underground stems that are squeezed into a short, broad, and fleshy package. Crocus and gladiolus are corms. If a corm bears small lateral buds on its surface, it only lasts one growing season, and a new corm is formed on top of the old, as in gladiolus. If the corm bears no lateral buds, like cyclamen, it will live from year to year, sending out new shoots to replace the old. It was knowing this simple fact, remembered from my botany classes, that led me to keep cyclamen corms growing all year instead of the old way of drying them every summer. Below is a gladiolus corm showing the tiny, lateral bud.

Bulbs are short stems wrapped in a series of leaves. If cut open lengthwise, you can see the embryo flower, already formed. Hyacinth and onion bulbs (1) are tightly encircled with leaves. Lily bulbs (2) have fewer and more fleshy leaves.

When a friend gives you a bag of unmarked bulbs, it's quite handy to know the differences. You might not get the genus and species but you can at least approximate the growing conditions.

Leaves

The typical leaf of a flowering plant consists of (1) the *blade* and (2) the stem, or *petiole*:

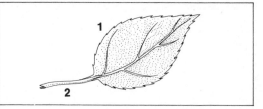

The undersurface of the leaf is covered by a network of *veins** which distribute food that is manufactured in the leaf to the rest of the plant, and carry water to the leaf cells. One of the primary methods of propagating the Rex begonias (see Chapter 5) consists of cutting the main veins of the leaves causing tiny plantlets to form. This is a relatively uncommon occurrence due to the presence of cellular tissue that is capable of further growth and development.

Leaves are arranged on the stem in three basic ways—(1) alternate, (2) opposite, and (3) whorled.

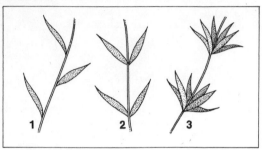

Next we have *simple* and *compound* leaves. Simple leaves consist of one blade, that is not divided, such as a geranium leaf:

Compound leaves come in two varieties. *Palmately compound*, where the leaflets are all attached to the stem at one place, as in the Virginia creeper (*Parthenocissus quinquefolia*);

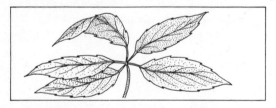

*These veins are used to distinguish the two great subdivisions of flowering plants: the *monocotyledons* and the *dicotyledons*. Dicotyledons generally have leaves with a complex shape, such as a maple leaf; the veining forms a definite criss-crossed network. Young seedlings have two leaves.

Monocotyledons have simpler leaf shapes and the veins run in a parallel manner. The young seedling has one leaf. From the standpoint of plant evolution, monocots are considered to be the more advanced form. Orchids, grasses, and lilies are examples of monocotyledons.

and *pinnately compound*, where the leaflets are arranged along a central stem as in the coffee plant (*Coffea arabica*):

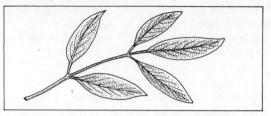

Now we come to leaf modifications. There are four major groupings, and each signals an important environmental need. *Succulent* leaves have developed a thick, fleshy form for storing water under desert conditions or to protect the leaves from long periods of drought. They require only minimum care, but must not be overwatered or placed in soils that offer inadequate drainage. Under wet conditions, their roots quickly rot. These roots are very fibrous, enabling them to absorb the smallest amount of moisture in the soil. If waterlogged, these thin roots quickly perish from lack of oxygen.

Spines are modified leaves found on most cacti. These plants evolved under desert conditions, as succulents, but found a different solution to the water problem. By adapting their stems to food manufacturing cacti have given up the wasteful job of growing new leaves each year. The leaves they possess have turned to fairly permanent spines and protect the precious stem from desert marauders. Cacti require the same soil conditions as succulents and lose their roots to disease in wet and soggy soils.

Tendrils of climbing plants are the third modification. They allow their weak-stemmed owners to climb just about anything available as they search for light. In clematis, the stem or petiole wraps itself about a support (see Chapter 7). In others, like smilax, the petiole divides on either side and forms a grasping tendril.

The fourth leaf modification is, without doubt, the most fantastic. These are the insectivorous plants. Because they grow in wet and boggy conditions, where soils are depleted in nitrogen and many other nutrients, the leaves have developed the ability to catch live food in the form of insects which act as a dietary supplement. The larger pitcher plants of the tropics can even digest small mice and birds. Strangely enough, since their leaves are abundantly supplied with chlorophyll, insectivores can manufacture sufficient food to exist, and even flower, without the addition of animal food, but growth and flowering is stimulated where insects are available (see Chapter 12).

Another leaf modification that generally goes unnoticed is the *bract.* Bracts are leaves that pretend to be flower petals when the plants' flowers are small and insignificant. The colorful display of poinsettias at Christmas is due not to flowers but to leaves that have turned into crimson flashes of color. In reality, dogwood flowers are tiny and the white "flowers" we enjoy are bracts (see Chapter 14).

Flowers

The present endpoint in plant evolution is evidenced by the flower, the only structure that is capable of producing seeds. Most people tend to ignore this biological aspect and think of floral beauty as purely an esthetic statement by nature. Since their beauty is entirely the result of an effort to attract insects for pollenation of the plant, it's extremely fortunate that we seem to have the esthetic sensibilities of the bee.[*]

All flowers are based on one general plan. Many have succeeded in hiding their similarities by structural changes, but the basic parts are there, if we look carefully enough. The following illustration shows the floral organs of a typical flower.

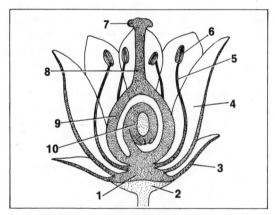

[*]Although we primarily think of the bee as the chief pollinator of flowers, other creatures are often involved. *Stapelia* spp. use flies (see Chapter 9); orchids are pollinated in nature by lizards, frogs, ants, beetles, flies, and bees; hummingbirds are the chief pollinators of columbine (see Chapter 11); butterflies pollinate many garden flowers; yucca cactus depends on a moth; and the hand of man is often used, completely replacing the pollinators of nature.

The *receptacle* (1) is attached to the plant stem by a special stalk known as the *pedicel* (2). The receptacle holds the *sepals* (3) which are collectively called the *calyx.* Occasionally sepals are brightly colored, as in tulips and lilies, but usually they are green. Sepals form a protective layer over the *petals* (4), which are usually brightly colored to form the initial attraction for insects, and are collectively called the *corolla.* Inside the corolla there are the *stamens* or male floral organs. The stamens consist of the *filament* (5) and the *anther* (6). The anther is the site of pollen formation. The female floral organ is called the *pistil* and is comprised of the *stigma* (7), which receives the pollen and is held by the *style* (8) which in turn is attached to the *ovary* (9) where the *ovules* (10) or seeds develop.

Pollinators, such as the bee, are attracted by the color and scent of the flower. Their goal is the nectar, produced by the flower. Usually nectar is made up of over 50 percent sugar and is the chief ingredient of honey. While searching flower after flower, the bee picks up bits of pollen that stick to the hairs on his body, mouth, and legs. Inadvertently, the bee deposits this pollen on flower stigmas, fertilization occurs, and ultimately seeds are produced.

Many flowers consist of both male and female floral organs and are called *complete* flowers. The lily is a prime example—many beautiful hybrids have been produced by cross-pollinating hybrids (see Chapter 13).

A few have separate male and female flowers on the same plant, as are found in the poinsettia (see Chapter 14).

The bittersweet vine of North America is an example of a plant that is either entirely male or female. Every year expectant gardeners wait in vain for the bright orange berries, because the nurseryman did not sell them two plants, one male (for the pollen) and one female (for the fruit).

When you have flowering house plants with complete flowers (both male and female) such as morning glories, you can do your own pollenating by dabbing the anther with a Q-Tip, or the like, and transferring the pollen to the stigma.

Some flowers refuse to be pollinated by their own pollen, and pollen from another plant of the same species must be used. The common day lily is a prime example, and many of the bromeliads will not self-pollinate.

At times the final result will be slightly disappointing as many of the large and beautiful flowers of today are hybrids, and each time you cross-pollinate, you travel back to the original flower and lose much of the impressive size and color. This is a fascinating hobby and many amateurs have come up with beautiful (and sometimes valuable) hybrids.

Multiple Flowers (Inflorescences)

Cyclamen, daffodils, and tulips are all examples of flowers that occur singly, and are called *solitary* flowers. In many types of plants, however, the typical flower is very small, and occurs in clusters called an *inflorescence*. This is an evolutionary adaptation to make the small flowers more easily visible to pollinators. There are many varieties of inflorescences, but the five most common types are:

1 A *head*, as found in the daisy and sunflower;

2 The *umbel*, typified by the onion family;

3 The *spike*, where the flowers are attached directly to the floral stem, such as gladiolus;

4 The *raceme* which resembles the spike, but where each flower is attached to the stem with pedicels, like the lily-of-the-valley and the hyacinth;

5 The *panicle*, characterized by the lilac and many of the bromeliads.

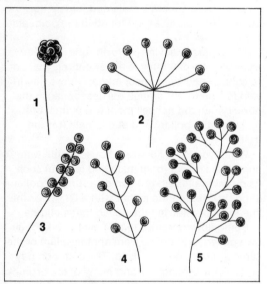

THE PLANT KINGDOM

When we look at a garden, formal park, or a greenhouse full of potted plants, we incorrectly assume that these are the main members of the plant world. The truth of the matter is much more complex, for petunias, pansies, orchids, and the like, belong to one group of a vast kingdom of plants comprising many divisions, almost all of which affect not only the health of our potted plants, but our very existence on earth. The knowledge that ferns are unlike flowering plants, that mildew prefers stagnant air, that green algae require bright light to thrive, allows us to understand conditions that not only affect the growth and development of our own plants, but affect disease as well.

The following are the major divisions of the plant kindom. You'll undoubtably run into examples of them all, whether by choice or misfortune.

Bacteria

These are the lowest on the ladder of plant evolution. They have but one cell, no roots, stems, or leaves, and no differentiation of sex. Bacteria cause untold death and destruction in the world: more people have died from infectious diseases than all wars and car accidents combined; but without them, not only would the toothpaste industry fall apart, the whole world would fall apart. For these are the plants that reduce the dead bodies of other plants and animals into the simple chemical compounds essential to all life on this earth. When we sterilize soils to prevent disease to potted plants, we stay short of complete sterilization in order to protect many of the helpful bacteria that inhabit soil (see Chapter 3). Among the most important are the nitrogen-fixing bacteria which convert the nitrogen found in organic remains (a nitrogen that cannot be absorbed by plants) into a different chemical form of nitrogen which is readily used by plants for nutrition.

Algae

Algae are very simple plant forms, though many have more than one cell. The giant sea kelps of the Pacific Ocean reach lengths of over 100 feet but are algal forms no more complex than the green scum that grows on sides of sunlit aquariums and terrariums. Algae point out the way home by growing on the north sides of trees in the deep woods, and give promise of supplying the world's hungry with needed proteins. However, when growing on the surface of potting soils or covering glass walls, they should be removed. They are danger signals of too-wet soils, improper fertilizing, and too much light. We'll cover this problem again in later chapters.

Fungi

Mushrooms, penicillin, mildew, yeast, wheat rust, and athlete's foot are all members of the fungus family. As a group, they do not have chlorophyll and must live by living on others. Occasionally, mushrooms and fungus will suddenly appear in terrariums, spores having entered with the soil or other plant life. They should not be allowed to remain, regardless of their temporary beauty, as plants of this sort quickly decay: mushrooms quickly turning into a liquid mess and fungus also decaying, soon after covering the more attractive members of the planting. Fungus and molds are particularly fond of damp, closed containers, with little light or air (see Chapter 15).

Lichens

Lichens are among the slowest growers in nature. In reality, they are a combination of an alga which produces the food, and a fungus which provides the living quarters. Some rock-growing lichens produce colonies barely half an inch high, three feet in diameter, and well over three hundred years old (see Chapter 6).

Liverworts and Mosses

These are the delicate plants of moist, shady areas under trees and in gardens and are collectively called the bryophytes. Sphagnum moss, when dried, is widely used to germinate seeds because of its ability to hold water and the fact that it's absolutely sterile when found in nature. Many moss beds act as miniature seed flats and if brought into the home terrarium, will suddenly sprout an endless variety of woodland plants. Liverworts need the same growing conditions as most mosses, but are not differenti-ated into leaves and stems, consisting instead of flattened fronds similar in shape to a one-dimensional liver. There is an additional difference between mosses and liverworts involving certain structures used in reproduction that are important to a botanist (see Chapter 6).

Ferns

Ferns are well known by everyone. They've been used as house plants since Victorian times. They are relatively undemanding, but differ from flowering plants by bearing spores, not seeds, on the undersides of their leaves. It's the one time when clusters of small, dark things are not insects or disease, but future members of the fern family (see Chapter 6).

Club Mosses

These are the trailing and creeping plants of the forest floor, resembling miniature pine trees. They are familiar to most people as Christmas decorations and are used to make wreaths. Unfortunately, unscrupulous people have stripped them from the forests of the northeast and they are scarcer than they were a generation ago.

Horsetail

These plants are often seen growing along railroad beds and in ditches along roadsides. Their stems are hollow with tiny, scalelike leaves above each joint. Because the stems contain high amounts of silica, they were used in pioneer days to scour pots and pans. I always keep a pot of them for interest and a conversation piece (see Chapter 6).

Conifers

The evergreen trees. They do not have flowers but release their pollen from unripened cones, which in turn bear the seeds. In the spring, dusting around our house consists of cleaning up unbelievable amounts of yellow dust that blows in the windows from the neighboring pines. While generally not kept as house plants, the many young seedlings make most interesting pot plants for a few years, or subjects for bonsai.

Flowering Plants

The present endpoint in plant evolution, flowering plants, comprises the majority of pot-plant subjects.

The illustration shows a somewhat fanciful terrarium, because in a well-managed set-up, the grower should be quick to remove the algae and fungi, but the other plants are all likely container subjects. Each member of the plant kingdom pictured is a primary example of its division:

1 Soil bacteria

2 Algae growing on the glass

3 Two members of the fungus division: (a) mold, (b) the tiny fairy mushroom

4 Lichens

5 Bryophytes (a) liverwort, (b) moss

6 Fern

7 Club moss

8 Horsetails

9 Conifers, represented by a white pine seedling.

10 Flowering plants, represented by a northeastern wild flower, the foamflower.

CHAPTER TWO
Constructing Window Greenhouses

In the past few years, the number of greenhouse manufacturers has steadily increased in the United States, and the once unglamorous, commercial greenhouse has undergone major redesigning. With the use of new materials of construction, greenhouses have become a valuable and esthetic addition to many American homes. For the homeowner with limited space or budget, trimly designed window greenhouses have appeared on the market; needing no foundations or major renovations, these units are easily attached to existing windows (see Chapter 16).

However, when attempting to construct a comparatively small area to house a plant collection, the individual who lives in a city apartment house or condominium faces major problems—in addition to budgetary considerations. Landlords resent any form of remodeling, including nail holes in plaster; city zoning and building codes usually prevent outside additions to buildings; fire departments resent blockage of fire-escapes; and the specter of home security is probably the greatest problem of all. Now add to these problems the fact that many apart-

ment dwellers are continually faced with the possibility of moving and cannot justify any large expense for the installation of permanent equipment.

Keeping these limitations in mind, here are two plans for indoor greenhouses, using the most inexpensive materials available and requiring only rudimentary knowledge of carpentry. In addition, they are portable, requiring only a few screws to hold them in place. If you should move, they can be easily disassembled, and the screw holes in window framing filled with plastic wood; the next tenant and the landlord will never even notice.

As we have noted before, two major factors involved in growing plants are the control of humidity and temperature. Many plants mentioned later (especially in Chapters 6 and 12), do best with humidity approximating that of the outdoors. Temperatures in the modern home, even with a cut in fuel deliveries, are still too high for many plants. The enclosures described in the following pages should enable you to provide more controls.

TOOLS REQUIRED

You'll need a hammer, screwdriver, a steel tape measure, polymer glue, an electric drill with a 7/32-inch and an 11/16-inch drill bit, a sharp saw or saber saw, and a framing square for right angles. Your ability to get along with the neighborhood lumber yard will be the deciding factor in needing additional tools, but we'll cover that contingency while discussing construction.

A FULL INDOOR WINDOW GREENHOUSE

The illustration shows all the details of construction, and is planned to fit around the window frame of an existing window. Lumber consists of standard one by twos, 3/4-inch AA plywood (exterior grade, since humidity will require waterproof glue) and 3/32-inch Lexan glazing—a clear plastic often used to replace window glass subject to continual breakage. All these materials are available at lumber yards, and if you're sure of your measurements, they will cut the plastic for you. At the time of this writing, Lexan costs about seventy-five to eighty cents a square foot. If you ask the lumber yard to cut it for you, the cost will probably be up to one dollar a square foot. It comes in a standard three-by-six foot stock size. Thicker grades are available, but

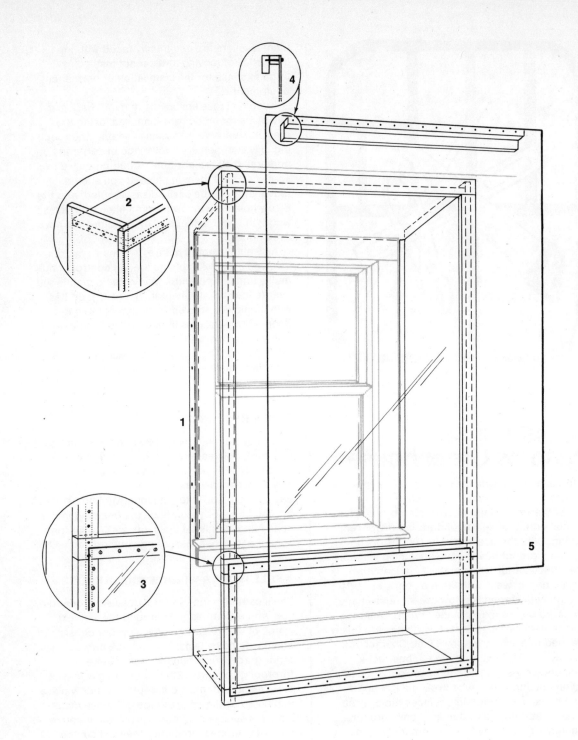

1

2

3

4

5

the cost goes up astronomically. If you do not have rapport with the men at the lumber yard or wish to save the cutting fee, you can cut this plastic sheeting yourself. Use a saber saw (with a fine-tooth blade) set at slow speed, or a hacksaw with a fine-tooth blade, or score the sheet with a utility knife, and break along the slice.

Screws are used instead of nails. I recommend using flat-head sheet-metal screws, size 10, 1 1/2-inches long, because the thread runs up to the screw head.

Obviously the plans should be modified to fit your window; just be careful with your measurements.

1 The basic frame is constructed of plywood. Fit a one-by-one spacer between the side and the window frame to avoid cutting around the window sill, and remember to remove a bit to fit around the baseboard. After the frame is finished, screw into the side of the window trim with 2½-inch size 10 screws, making a hole with a 7/32-inch bit.

2 The top piece of the frame is dropped at least an inch to provide clearance for the wooden brace that holds the plastic front in place. The front of the frame is finished with one by twos.

3 Since the Lexan comes no larger than six feet long, if you're making a large unit, this bottom piece of Lexan, screwed to the one by two's enables you to keep the front clear. Drill holes in the plastic, using the 7/32-inch bit, and 3/4-inch size 10 screws.

4 The brace for the Lexan doubles as the wooden hook, holding the plastic in place. Use a one by one topped with a one by two. Use the 7/32-inch bit and drill holes, then screw with 1½-inch size 10 screws, adding a rubber washer before tightening each screw.

Lexan comes covered with plastic film to protect it during shipment. Remove only enough of this film to give you clearance for working. Wait until you are done to remove the rest, as this plastic scratches easily.

Paint the inside with a white, waterproof paint to give added reflection of light. Add aluminum cookie or baking pans to the bottom, and fill them with gravel and water for humidity.

Using your imagination, you can most likely arrive at many different applications of this basic design. You could add lighting if your window is not particularly bright, or by using light fixtures alone, you can construct the unit in a dark corner (see Chapter 1 and Bibliography).

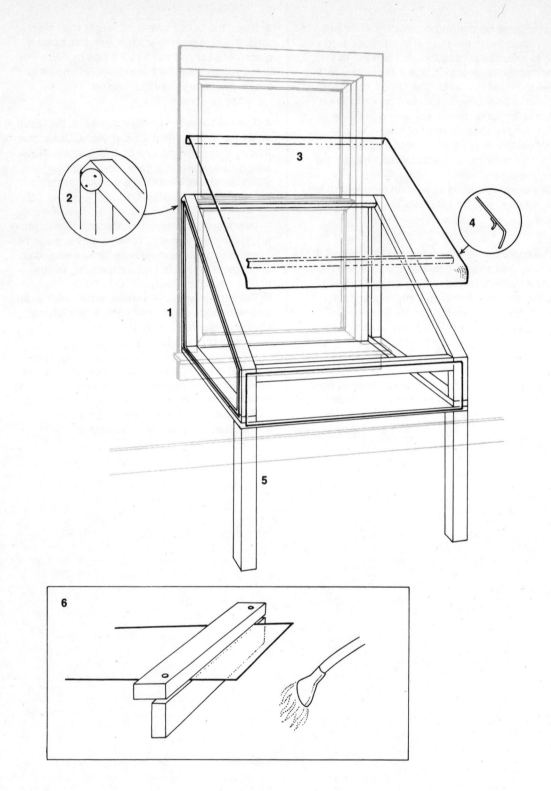

A SMALL PLASTIC WINDOW GARDEN

The same basic materials are used for this unit as in the first.

1 The basic frame is made of one by twos, with a plywood bottom that will rest on the window sill, affixed with two screws when the unit is finished.

2 The side-frame angles are figured with your eye or a sliding T-head from the hardware store. They can be screwed, nailed, or held together with tops from frozen orange juice cans and two 4d nails. The Lexan is cut to size and screwed onto the frame. Two cross pieces of one by two are screwed on with 1½-inch No. 8 sheet-metal screws. The frame is screwed to the plywood bottom. A front piece of Lexan is screwed onto the frame and the front edge of the plywood bottom.

3 In order to hold the plastic top, it is bent with the application of heat. This forms a good seal and adds rigidity to the plastic.

4 A small plastic strip is glued to the bottom of the cover to catch condensation which will drip into the unit instead of on the floor.

5 Legs consist of two two by threes. They can be nailed, screwed, or hinged.

6 This shows the set-up for bending the plastic. Two one by twos and two 6d nails hold the plastic sheet in place. For heat use a propane torch. Three hundred degrees F. is enough to soften this plastic, so never get the flame too close. If the wood starts to char, you *are* too close! Pass the torch back and forth where it leaves the wooden frame. When the plastic starts to drop down, press it with a dry rag or piece of wood, and when the desired angle is reached, rub the crease with a wet paper towel to cool it. If you don't hold the sheet down as it cools, it will revert to its original shape.

Any sharp edges can be filed and sanded to smoothness.

Most hobby shops now stock equipment for bending plastic. They're called heating strips, and are very easy to use.

SHELVING FOR PLANTS

Endless methods for making shelving are now on the general market, but the following two ideas give finished and attractive results with little investment, plus they allow free circulation of air.

The first shelf is made from 1/2- or 3/4-inch EMT metallic electrical tubing. It's smooth and galvanized both inside and out for protection against water. I prefer the 3/4-inch for added stability.

Take a one by three and drill holes with a 15/16-inch bit, keeping the holes in a straight line. Cut the piece exactly in half and then screw to either end of your unit. Now cut the tubing into the correct length, using a fine-toothed hacksaw or a cheap plumber's tubing cutter, which still retails for about two dollars.

Or make a floor bench using two by tens or two by twelves of pine (redwood is great if you can afford it). Use a 15/16-inch drill bit for the

holes. The tubing comes in ten-foot lengths, so that's the limit to size. Use three pieces of wood for strength.

To secure the tubing from moving, use a 5/64-inch twist drill and drill a hole from the top of the wooden supports, down through each tube, and drop in a 4d nail.

Another great bench is very simply made from #2 grade pine one by two's (#2 means the wood has knots, but it's much cheaper than #1), galvanized finishing nails, size 4d, and glue. Bunch a number of one by twos and cut a large number of spacers at one time, about three inches long. Nail and glue three spacers (more, if you are making a bench longer than six feet) to a piece of one by two. Now just continue the process until it's as large as you want it. To finish it off, use a router for rounding the edges, and paint with three thin coats of marine varnish, sanding with fine sandpaper between each coat. I've had a set of these benches for over three years, constantly exposed to water, and they're still in perfect shape.

For legs, use aluminum legs from the hardware store, or four lengths of 3/4-inch pipe threaded into pipe flanges that are screwed to the base; or make saw horses from two by fours and folding metal clamps made for this purpose.

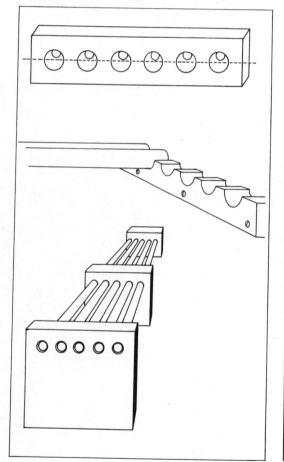

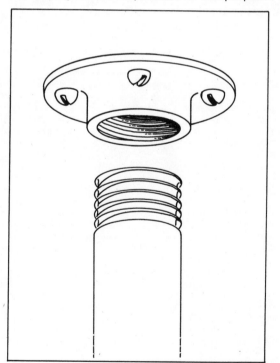

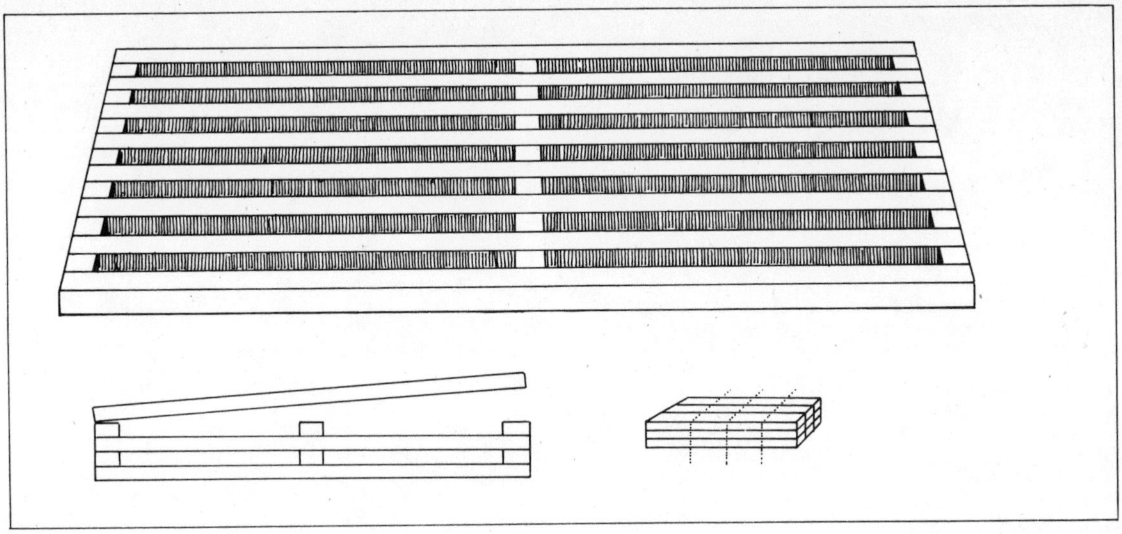

CHAPTER THREE
Down to Earth

The purpose of soil is to hold up the plant and provide it with air, water, and nourishment through a healthy root system. As we have seen earlier, the soil must be porous enough to allow for the entry of air, the passage of water, and to provide minerals for the plant. Because the requirements for plants differ according to their native environmental needs I have devised a number of individualized potting mixes which are referred to in the cultural instructions. While backyard soil might be great for weeds and grasses, it's not particularly suited to a jungle fern or barrel cactus.

Potting Sheds

If you have any available space, it's always an excellent idea to set up a potting shed. Nothing fancy—just an area where soil can be mixed in advance and stored in marked containers and pots stacked for future use; then if some dirt winds up on the floor, nobody gets too upset. I know from personal experience that mixing soils can get messy. A common place for tools is also needed, so the endless walks from room to room, looking for one small item, can be avoided.

POTTING MIXES

The following is a list of the readily available items that may be used to prepare a soil mix:

• Aquarium gravel, found in pet shops, comes in many colors as well as sand-colored or white. It's a great item to keep on hand, especially if the sand bank is frozen solid.

• Bird gravel can be bought in pet shops or super markets. It's a tooth substitute for birds, but once again, handy to use in lieu of sand.

• Charcoal is another aquarium supply item. It's used to keep soil from becoming rank, by absorbing obnoxious odors from decaying vegetation, especially where soil is moist or wet, as in terrariums. I've always used it as it's been cheap up to now. Since I've not been bothered with odors, I assume it works.

• Humus is the residue of the compost heap. It is well-decomposed vegetation that is black, sweet-smelling, loose in texture, and a marvelous material for plants.

• Leaf mold, which is natural compost from the forest floor, is a very desirable addition to soil mixes because of its high organic content from decaying plant material. When gathered under evergreens, it's on the acid side; from hardwoods, tends toward the alkaline.

• Loam is the catch-all word for good garden soil containing clay, sand, and humus.

• Osmunda is made from the roots of the cinnamon fern (*Osmunda cinnamomea*) and has for years been considered the one material for growing orchids because it has organic value. Today it is rarely used by big commercial growers because of relatively high costs, and tree bark is used instead, although plants grown in bark require additional fertilizers. Osmunda is used with many epiphytes, such as bromeliads, and can also cover drainage holes in clay pots when you can't find a piece of crockery.

• Perlite is made from volcanic rock that is commercially perked in a giant pressure cooker. It has no nutritive value, but helps to aerate heavy soils.

• Peat, sold by bag or bale, is the organic residue of many different kinds of plants that have become decomposed in water. Sphagnum moss may form part of its content, but never all.

• Peat moss is partially decomposed sphagnum moss that will loosen a hard-packed soil, add nutritive value as it continues to decompose, is on the acid side, and a chore to moisten if it is completely dried out. Pour boiling water on it, allow to cool, and squeeze out the excess moisture.

• Sand is one of the main constituents of a good soil, since it helps to make heavy soils more porous. Use builder's sand or sharp sand, being sure to wash it before use. "Sharp" simply means that the sand grains are rough to the touch, as opposed to soft sand which is generally too fine to be useful. Beach sand is too full of salt and is also soft.

• Sphagnum moss identifies several different kinds of mosses that grow in bogs and swamps, spreading rapidly as they grow. The older parts below turn into peat moss. It's extensively used to germinate seedlings and as a growing medium for bog plants. It's acidic and when milled or pulverized is just as hard to moisten as peat.

• Store-bought soil is fine for part of a mix, but the cheaper types pack down too readily and the better varieties are just too expensive compared to the cost of mixing your own. Always keep a bag around for emergencies.

• Vermiculite, a very lightweight material made from expanded mica, is useful for growing seedlings and to break up heavy soils. I use it for a soil replacement in combination with special pots for water or soil-less culture. Vermiculite is also sold by the bag for insulating house walls, but this kind consists of very large pieces that are not too workable for the indoor gardener.

The following are listed separately because they are more readily identified as fertilizers, but are not made from chemicals. We'll discuss chemical fertilizers later in the chapter.

• Bone meal is a good old-fashioned source of phosphorus especially liked by bulbs and cactus. It is slow acting and organic. Superphosphate, manufactured commercially, is faster acting and more powerful.

• Chicken manure should not be used by a heavy hand, especially when fresh, as the nitrogen content is so high that the roots may get first-degree burns.

• Cow manure should also not be used when fresh. When composted it is a welcome addition to soil mixes. It has slightly less nitrogen than sheep manure and for obvious reasons relating to production, is slightly cheaper.

• Dried blood is found with the manures in garden shops. It's supposed to keep rabbits and deer away from outdoor gardens but does not faze them in the least. It has a lot of nitrogen but I believe that the manures are better.

• Eggshells are a very good and ready source of calcium, about which more later.

• Sheep manure can be used when composted. It has a bit more nitrogen than cow manure and is more expensive.

• Wood ashes are a good source of potassium, sometimes called potash. Potash is the term for potassium compounds, and can be gathered from the fireplace.

These definitions cover about everything needed to make good soil mixes. The cultural instructions given later in this book mention a correct type of potting soil for each plant. The following formulas are for general use. *

All-purpose mix for general potting where specific requirements are not given:
1/4 loam or packaged soil
1/4 sand
1/4 leaf mold or peat moss
1/4 composted manure
Depending on the amount you are making, add up to a pint of bone meal for a bushel of soil.

Tropical plant mix:
1/4 loam or packaged soil
1/2 leaf mold or peat moss
1/4 sand

*If you have an unidentified plant, and have no idea where it came from, examine it closely and you will be able to judge what type of soil to use: Plants with fibrous roots, thin leaves, and weak, flexible stems will do well in the all-purpose mix; plants with heavier stems, thicker roots and/or aerial roots, and substantial leaves with a slight gloss should go in the tropical plant mix; plants with very thick, fleshy leaves, thorns, and heavy stems probably belong in the cactus and succulent mix.

Cactus and succulents:
1/4 loam or packaged soil
1/4 leaf mold or peat moss
1/4 sand
1/4 gravel or small pieces of broken pots
Depending on the amount, add up to a pint of
bone meal per bushel of soil.

Terrarium mix:
1/4 humus or leaf mold
1/4 sphagnum moss
1/4 peat moss
1/4 sand and gravel

SOIL-LESS MIXES

There has been a new development in the past
few years that may meet your soil needs. It's
called the soil-less mix. The basic ingredients
are inert mineral and organic derivatives with
the addition of nutrients. Although the recipes
look as though you must have a chemist's de-
gree to put them together, the ingredients are
readily available at garden centers and the drug
store, and easy to keep on hand. They were developed at the New York State College of Agriculture at Cornell University to help commercial
growers, but are easily adaptable to home use.
They are particularly recommended to the city
dweller who doesn't have sufficient working
space or sources for soil, and the fact that
spilled mix is cleanly vacuumed up has much to
recommend it. Roof gardeners take note, as the
mixes are very light in weight.

The measurements below will each make one
bushel of mix.

Cornell Foliage Plant Mix:

1/2 bushel	Sphagnum peat moss
1/4 "	Vermiculite, No. 2
1/4 "	Perlite (medium fine)
8 tablespoons	Ground dolomitic limestone
2 "	Superphosphate (20% powdered)
3 "	10-10-10 Fertilizer
1 "	Iron sulfate
1 "	Potassium nitrate

This foliage plant mix is well suited for ferns,
amaryllis, begonias, cissus, citrus, coleus,
oxalis, pilea, sansevieria, and tolmiea.

Cornell Epiphytic Mix:

1/3 bushel	Douglas fir bark (fine grind)
1/3 "	Sphagnum peat moss (shredded)
1/3 "	Perlite (medium fine)
8 tablespoons	Ground dolomitic limestone
6 "	Superphosphate (20% powdered)
3 "	10-10-10 Fertilizer
1 "	Iron sulfate
1 "	Potassium nitrate

The epiphytic plant mix is suited to bromeliads, episcias, hoya, monstera, nephytis, po-
tohos, and syngonium.

A supplemental application of a water-soluble
fertilizer—a 20-20-20 formula—should be given
once a month (described later). Plants growing
in full sun should receive about one third more
fertilizer than those grown in the shade. During
winter months in the north, only about half the
amount should be used.

STERILIZATION OF SOIL

Anyone making their own soil mixes should be
sure that the ingredients are free from disease.
This is especially true of soils gathered in the
garden or the woods. Not only does soil harbor
beneficial bacteria, but also a host of other little
pests, including insect eggs. You can spend an
hour with a hand lens on one square foot of
woods litter and have a constant parade of little
beings that would thoroughly enjoy an epicure's
vacation on a house plant. There are two general methods of sterilizing soil—heat or chemicals.
It has been said that the odor of baking soil
does the family an injustice. Perhaps if your
group is a bit sensitive it's noticeable, but it's
soon gone and not repellent in quality. On the
other hand, the chemical most frequently used
for soil sterilization is formalin, which is 40 percent formaldehyde and is extremely dangerous
to have about the house. The odor is not only
repellent but *ghastly*. Naturally, I recommend
the oven method.

Spread moist, not dry, soil on a baking or
cookie sheet and heat the soil for fifteen minutes
at 185° Fahrenheit or 83° Centigrade. Use a
candy thermometer to check temperatures. This
heat will kill fungus, insects, and weed seeds
without harming the beneficial bacteria.

FERTILIZERS

Before discussing fertilizers for your plants, remember one axiom: Don't overdo it! We all have a tendency to try to make a good thing better; that's a natural part of the human condition, but it's one thing to achieve a tenfold increase in corn yield or produce the biggest cabbage in the world, earning a place in the *Guiness Book of Records*, and quite another to bombard a helpless pot plant with too much food. Since most of us don't have the room for giant plants to begin with, especially as our collecting mania soon fills all available space, it's better to keep a plant in good condition rather than making it bend at the ceiling. Certainly some feeding is a desirable thing, but if our potting mixes are correctly suited to the particular plant, it doesn't take much food to keep it healthy.

Plants need three elements for healthy growth, and a number of trace elements in minor amounts. The big three are nitrogen, phosphorus, and potassium.

Nitrogen is beneficial to the healthy growth of shoots and leaves. It's absolutely necessary for forming a plant's supply of chlorophyll. Without nitrogen the plant's growth is restricted, the root system becomes stunted and the leaves yellow and fall off. However, too much nitrogen results in an excessive leaf growth (at the expense of flowers) and long, spindly stems.

Phosphorus helps a plant to develop flowers and healthy roots and to resist many diseases. Without it, lower leaves yellow and drop off and yellow edges develop on the upper leaves.

Potassium acts as a balance between the other two; it delays the maturing, undue ripening effect of phosphorus and it slows the tendency to overgrowth caused by nitrogen. When potassium is lacking, leaves turn dry and scorched around the edges.

(Most of these symptoms can be caused by other factors such as temperature, improper watering, and disease, so check these first before increasing fertilizers.)

Good plant foods are measured in percentages of these three elements. A typical formula would be 5-10-5: 5 percent nitrogen, 10 percent phosphorus, and 5 percent potassium. It doesn't add up to 100 percent because these chemicals are so powerful that a large amount of neutral substances have been added to the mix. These percentages can easily be varied, and large feed and fertilizer concerns will mix any formula one could want. But we're dealing with house plants

and not jumbo rye, so unless your soils are woefully bad to begin with, or you're experimenting on a big scale, stick to something simple. In order to cut down on the general complications of life, I use a standard 20-20-20 formula for established plants, and a 10-10-10 (the same but a weaker formula) for seedlings. In addition, I always cut the mixing directions by half, just to be on the safe side. The trace elements that were mentioned previously as necessary to good growth, are usually added to the better commercially prepared mixes.

Keep away from gimmicks like pills and capsules that are buried in the soil. They release chemicals whenever you water, whether the plant needs it or not, and once implanted are a bit difficult to remove.

A few rules:

1 Don't feed a plant when it's blooming. The very fact that it is flowering means you were doing the right thing to begin with, so it's best to stop until blooming is over. If the plant is a long-term bloomer, just slow down the applications.

2 Don't feed when plants are resting or dormant, especially during the winter months up north.

3 Don't flood an absolutely dry soil with fertilizer. The roots are tender and could suffer from burning. This isn't likely when foods are diluted enough, but it's a good habit to get into.

4 Actively growing plants need more food than slowpokes, but don't feed if there is not evidence of growth.

5 Don't feed a plant that is suffering from a disease.

6 If your pots have a healthy growth of algae on their sides, or the top of the soil exhibits a white, granular aspect, the chances are the plants are getting too much food.

After repotting, I generally wait a good six months before beginning applications, then I apply weak solutions every three weeks or so.

If any plant has a specific feeding demand, check the cultural instructions.

pH

pH is a term consistently bandied about by indoor and outdoor gardeners, but is very rarely explained to anyone's satisfaction. It has the aura of chemistry so we either go overboard and test everything we can get our trowels into or completely ignore it in hopes it will go away. Unfortunately, it's important to the health of a great many plants. True, some will survive in improperly balanced soils, but it often spells the difference between luxuriant growth and just bare survival.

Literally pH means the potential for hydrogen or hydroxyl ions in the soil.* Practically it's a test to determine the relative acidity, or sourness, and alkalinity, or sweetness, of soil.

Every time it rains, the action of water washes out accumulations of elements in the soil. One of these elements is calcium and, as it disappears, soil becomes more acidic. It's an extremely slow process in nature but over the years definite patterns of soil type have developed throughout any region. Swamps and bogs that have high percentages of peat are extremely acidic; in humid regions, and most woods and forests, the soil is moderately acidic to slightly alkaline; arid regions go from slightly moderate to a strong alkaline content; and desert areas in the southwest of the United States have vast alkali flats.

The chart below is a measure in units of 3 to 11. Neutral soil is 7 and most plants grow between ranges of 4.5 and 7.5.

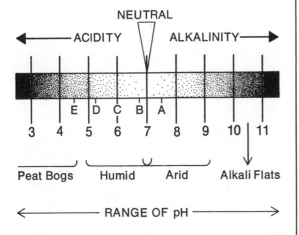

*The chemical formula for water is H_2O. The molecules of water ionize slightly into hydrogen ions with a positive charge (H+) and hydroxyl ions with a negative charge (OH-). Hydrogen ions are acid and hydroxyl ions are alkaline. Because equal numbers of the ions are formed for each molecule of water, water is acidic, basic and neutral. On the logarithmic scale of pH, pure water is pH 7, or neutral. Alkaline solutions or soil contain less hydrogen ions and more hydroxyl ions; acid soils are just the reverse.

Each unit up and down the scale is measured in a tenfold increase or decrease from point 7. Four would be 1,000 times as acid as 7; 9 would be 100 times as alkaline.

By comparing the letter code in the following list to the pH chart, you can see the amount of variations found in this sampling of flowering plants grown in and around the home. A complete list of plants and their pH rating is in the Appendix.

Plant	Code	Plant	Code
African violet	B	Hydrangea, Blue	E
Ageratum	B	" Pink	C
Amaryllis	D	Lily	C
Avocado	B	Morning glory	A
Banana	B	Nasturtium	A
Begonia	C	Orchid	D
Calendula	A	Petunia	A
Clematis	A	Pitcher plant	E
Cyclamen	C	Rhododendron	E
Daisy	B	Star of Bethlehem	B
Fuchsia	B	Tulip	B
Gardenia	C	Zinnia	B
Heliotrope	A		

Years ago, pH was not considered to be very important in raising house plants. Greenhouse gardeners with the responsibilities of huge and valuable commercial crops were aware of the soil demands of their charges, but the typical house-plant enthusiasts were generally unaware of pH. They knew through trial and error that certain soils worked for certain plants. Varieties were few, but their begonias, geraniums and ivies were beautiful. When visiting your friends and admiring their plants, quite often you'd get a present of a plant or a cutting. "What do I pot it in," you'd ask. "Oh, just about any dirt will do," came the reply. Talk would then turn to the problems of the day, and just as you would leave, a voice would cry out: "Oh, by the way, remember to add a few crushed eggshells to the soil every so often!"

Grandmother had the secret. Eggshells are a fine source of calcium. By crushing the shells and adding a pinch to the soil surface, she had paraphrased today's "tiny, time capsules" which release small and continuous amounts of calcium, offsetting the natural acidity of soils. Since most house plants prefer between 6 and 7.5 on the pH scale, healthy plants were the result.

Except in our more modern kitchens, eggshells are still available. Collect them, air dry them, and pulverize them in the blender. If you have an old-time mortar and pestle and a willing wrist, it works eminently well or simply fold the shells in a newspaper and attack with a rolling pin. Just add a generous pinch of crushed eggshells to the soil every few months.

The obvious time to check pH is when working with a healthy plant at the time of repotting or when dealing with native plants brought in from the woods and fields. By looking at the pH preferences of some typical plants, you will see some notable exceptions to the general range of 7.5 to 6. The acid preferences of bog plants and insectivores or the alkaline demands of cactus would produce an unhealthy zinnia or heliotrope. Also, while generalizations can be made concerning soils around the United States, there are wide fluctuations on the local levels.

There are two fine testing kits for pH on the market today. The Sudbury Soil Testing Kit is complete and perfect, both for the amateur chemist and the purist. Not only can you check pH, but the soil content of nitrogen, phosphorus, and potassium. The other kit is a variation on litmus paper, a dyed paper strip made from, of all things, lichens. It reacts by color to pH and comes in a small plastic casette. Made by the Perfect Garden Company, it's too handy not to have.

We've talked about the acid content of soils, but what about moving an alkaline soil down the pH scale to the acid range? This condition is not very common but if it does occur, the addition of aluminum sulfate or alum salts to the potting mix will solve the problem. It's best to get one of the pH kits and follow their instructions rather than use a hit or miss application of chemicals.

We are not finished with pH yet. It affects not only soil but water. Soft water is generally free of mineral salts and leaves the bathtub ring-free. It's acid in reactions and the best source is rainwater. Hard water is alkaline and has heavy concentrations of calcium and other minerals. Soap forms curds in hard water.

Now, you ask, didn't we just finish adding calcium to the soil to offset its acidity? Yes, but in small amounts. When watering with hard water, we continually add these salts, day after day, and it's not too long before the soil becomes so saturated that a dull, gray film will form on the leaves of many plants that is unattractive and cuts down on available light. Since hard water can be softened by boiling (thus leaving the mineral salts in the kettle) or using rainwater, it's easy to control. Better to limit your problems to the soil and forget the additional worry of hard water. Don't use water softened by commercial water softeners. They exchange the calcium for sodium, and while the water becomes kind to your hair, it slowly kills the plants. This does not happen overnight. Slowly the plants become stunted in growth and, if unchecked, eventually die.

CHAPTER FOUR
Pots and Potting

ESTHETICS OF POTS

Unfortunately there are two words synonymous with pots. One is clay, the other is plastic. Clay is a time-honored material with a long cultural history; plastic is a Frankenstein's monster, conceived in the thirties, and now out of control.

When our descendants search the rubbish piles of today, a thousand years hence, not only will they find beer cans, throw-away bottles, and cutesy deodorant containers, but they will dig up millions of plastic flower pots, many with imitation 14-carat-gold rims.

No one would dare to frame a Rembrandt or van Gogh in a plastic frame studded with gold flecks and jazzy rhinestones, except perhaps in a Las Vegas hotel. Then why put a real plant, the creation of millions of years of evolution, into an imitation clay pot with a cornflower decal?

Plastic and styrofoam pots work well for the commercial grower who has skyrocketing maintenance costs and who must meet deadlines for seasonal markets that are as hectic as the fashion industry. He has an excuse to use such pots because they *are* cheaper; his plants are grown on schedules and are in essence manufactured on an assembly-line basis, like cars and T.V.'s. But you can easily remove the plant from its artificial container when you reach home. (I suggest using plastics in this and other sections of the book, but generally they are imported plastics which serve a function that cannot be achieved in clay.)

There are good reasons other than esthetic ones for using clay containers. Clay "breathes," allowing air and water to pass through the walls. It's much more difficult to overwater when using clay. I'm convinced that more damage is done by lethal overwatering to house plants growing in plastic pots than any other mistreatment known. Furthermore, clay is much heavier and keeps larger plants from toppling in a mild breeze when outside or falling over because you brushed against it in the home. Clay will last much longer (as long as you don't continually drop pots) than plastic, which becomes brittle with age. By looking at the algae or salt deposits forming on the clay, you have an early warning system that predicts problems long before the plant itself shows signs of trouble.

An empty clay pot can sit alone on a shelf and make an esthetic statement. A whoopy-do plastic zinger of a pot speaks harshly for itself.

CLAY POTS

Clay pots are made in many different sizes and shapes. They start at 2 inches, measured by the diameter across the top, and go up to 16 inches or more. Their height is about the same as the diameter. Many have names long associated with English gardens. The 2-inch pot is called the "thimble," the 2 1/2-inch pot the "thumb." When the height exceeds the diameter they're called "long Toms;" when shorter than they are wide they are called "dwarfs." You'll also find azalea pots which are three quarters of the standard depth, allowing for shallower root systems.

I rarely find a use for the thimble and thumb pots because they are so small; the soil dries out too quickly, but they're fun to have around for an extra small cactus or a conversation piece. It's difficult to believe that one can make a pot so small. Before peat pots and Jiffy-7's were developed, these small pots were extensively used for seedlings. Now we transplant the beginning seedlings and their peat pots into three-inch clay when the plants are big enough. Depending on the age of the pot and the manufacturer, you'll find minor variations in the thickness of the clay walls and top measurements.

New clay pots are bone dry and must be thoroughly soaked in water before use, or they'll quickly draw most of the water from the soil. Old and reused pots must be cleaned and scrubbed. Steel wool will easily remove an accumulation of mineral salts.

Drainage holes are found in the bottom. These should be covered with a few shards of broken pot to keep soil from escaping and, if your plants are outside or in a greenhouse, a small piece of screening to guard against wandering slugs and other undesirables.

Never paint pots. If you want to make an attractive display for a beautiful plant, find a suitable jardinaire or other container and place the clay pot within.

POTTING

When a plant needs repotting, it's only moved up one size, at the most two. A small plant in a large pot not only looks rather strange; it usually does not last too long. Unless plant roots extend throughout the soil, the excess becomes soggy and compacted leading to sickly growth.

Repotting becomes necessary when the roots completely occupy all the soil and the root ball assumes the shape of the pot. The first sign is roots working their way through drainage holes. The best time for repotting is early spring when plants begin active root growth after a winter's rest. The worst time is during winter, because broken roots have a smaller chance of healing quickly before disease can set in. An actively growing plant can be repotted at any time.

If you are worried about a plant being potbound you can easily check without hurting it. Place two fingers, one on either side of the stem to hold the soil and flip the pot over. Rap it on a

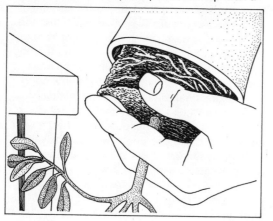

hard edge and the soil ball should slide out. Wait until the plant's soil is fairly dry for this routine; soaking wet soil will fight you all the way.

If all looks okay, and the roots are not massed on the outside, pop the plant back in the pot. If not, move up to the next size.

Take your larger pot, crock it, sprinkle some new soil on the bottom and place the root ball on top. Sprinkle new soil about the sides and give the pot a sharp thump on a table or the floor to help settle the soil. Firm the edges with your thumbs and the job's done.

One important thing to remember: leave enough room at the top of the pot for watering. With a five-inch pot, there should be at least a three-quarter inch clearance between the rim and the soil. Nothing is quite so aggravating as watering a plant, dribbling mud down the pot side, then having to go at it again because in the first attempt the plant got half and the floor got the rest.

After potting, water the plant well to help in settling the soil. If you packed it a bit on the loose side, you'll notice a few depressions. Just sprinkle some more soil in them to level the surface. I always add a small shard or flat stone to the surface to break the force of water when it leaves the watering can.

When watering a plant, the pot sits in a saucer to catch the excess water. If there is no room between the water and the pot bottom, the water seeps back in. This is fine with many plants, but some resent it. Set the pot on a few pebbles, or large pieces of gravel, and make sure the saucer is large enough to take the water without overflowing. The slow evaporation from the saucer will add to humidity and save the time devoted to emptying saucers after watering.

Root Pruning

Sometimes you have a plant that is obviously potbound; yet you feel that both plant and pot are large enough and you would like to maintain status quo for a time.

Remove the root ball and set it on your work surface. Take a large, sharp knife and slice off about half an inch of soil and roots. Then repot as before adding new soil around the edges. Then prune the plant itself slightly. Don't overdo it. Since the plant just lost some roots that were obviously in use, make its job a bit easier by giving it less top growth to supply with water and such.

Top Dressing

Suppose you have a truly potbound plant, no extra pots and no time to become overly involved with potting. Remove about an inch of the surface soil and replace it with new potting mix. As you water, the freshened soil will help the roots along and stave off the inevitable for a while. Occasionally the pot will break from the pressures of the roots, and you'll be forced to repot it.

SELF-WATERING POTS

I've made my position against plastic pots very clear, but I'm allowed a few exceptions—the Riviera self-watering pots. Made in France of molded plastic in attractive colors, this device allows you to be an absentee plantlord without worry. A nylon fabric held by a plastic grid supports the soil and provides water from a reservoir with a nylon wick. The soil grid is held above the water level by a hollow tube that allows a continuous flow of air to reach the root system. If the reservoir is filled and the plant located in a cool, well-ventilated spot, you can leave home for at least three weeks. By covering the topsoil with aluminum foil, you can stay away even longer.

By adding fertilizer to the water, and using a soil-less mix of vermiculite and peat moss, many plants grow beautifully as hydroponic subjects.

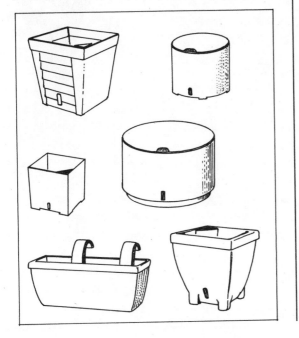

The pots are available in many variations, from small to large planters, troughs, flats, and hanging-balcony troughs.

There are other self-watering pots on the market today, but from my point of view, they are either too ugly or they work on the principle of a pot sitting directly on a wick or spongy surface. This you can easily do on your own, so why bother? Also, wicks inserted through the drainage hole cut off air circulation to the bottom of the pot.

A water wick is manufactured by Mardon Gardens that works through the soil surface. One end is placed in a glass of water and the other inserted into the soil. It works on capillary action but is not advised for plants that like dry soil, or plants that require a dry period between each watering.

Since a great many people are insulating their houses today, those hardier folk could take some excess fiberglass and weave their own wicks. Personally, I've had enough of fiberglass slivers in my hands and hair. I'll purchase the wicks outright.

Pots Without Drainage Holes

You might have an especially attractive container around the house that you'd love to use for a decorative plant, but the pot has no drainage holes and you're worried about overwatering. Here's a solution that really works. At any store that sells tropical fish, buy a piece of plastic tubing the height of your pot. Set it within the pot in an upright position and add between two and three inches of coarse gravel, making sure the tube hits the bottom. Add the appropriate soil mix and pot the plant, watering it fully. Using a wooden dowel as a dipstick, measure the water supply periodically; when the stick comes out completely dry, water again.

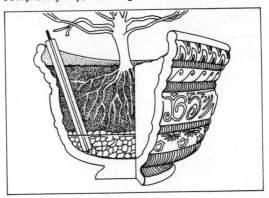

Pots Within Pots

If you have a plant you wish to display in a fancy waterproof container for a short time, cover the bottom of the container with a few inches of perlite and set the pot on top. The excess water will collect in the perlite, slowly evaporating, adding to the humidity and keeping the plant from soggy soil. If the container is large enough, a clean brick or a piece of two-by-four lumber will do.

If the plant you wish to display does best in moist soil, try this. Take your container and set the pot on a few inches of shards or clean stones. Pack the sides with sphagnum moss. The water from the wet moss will seep through the porous clay walls and keep the soil consistently moist, not soggy.

NOTE: In the other chapters in this book, through written description and illustrations, I've attempted to show as many variations and ideas on pots that I could manage. Like the frames on a picture, each plant deserves its own particular container.

The full page drawing shows a group of plants that have been growing in a six-inch Riviera pot for well over a year. Liquid fertilizer (20-20-20) is applied once a month:

1 Chinese evergreen, *Aglaonema simplex*

2 *A. commutatum* 'Malay Beauty'

3 *A. commutatum elegans*

4 Satin pothos, *Scindapsus pictus argyraeus*

5 Devil's ivy, *S. aureus*

CHAPTER FIVE
Seeds and Cuttings

Sooner or later, after becoming involved with growing plants, the collecting urge appears from left field and we begin to wish for more. When the urge strikes but the pocketbook rebels, the best and easiest solution is to grow your own plants from seed. In addition to being one of the easiest methods, it enables you to try many new kinds of plants, ordinarily unavailable from the majority of commercial nurseries.

Most of the major seed companies now offer seed-starter kits that are almost foolproof, and an ever-increasing selection of house-plant seeds are available (see Appendix). Since so many varieties of equipment are offered and the selection is basically a personal choice, I'm just going to deal with the methods that I use.

As a seed-growing medium, sphagnum moss is my first choice. It's tidy and free of contaminating organisms. Furthermore, nonsterile mediums tend to favor the development of a fungus growth that destroys seedlings as they emerge from the ground in a process called *damping-off*. Either gather your own moss from a local swamp (see Chapter 6), allow it to air-dry, and shred it into tiny pieces with your hands, or buy milled sphagnum from the local nursery.

"Milled" simply means that the shredding has been done for you. The disease organisms that cause damping-off are found in soils, so you do not have to worry when using moss.

For seed-growing containers, I use either peat pots or Jiffy-7's. Peat pots are good for small sowings when I intend to transplant the seed-

lings at a later date. If seeds are large, like nasturtiums or morning glories, and will go from germination to potting without a transplant step, Jiffy-7's are perfect. They come flat for easy storage, but by adding water, they quickly increase to their proper size.

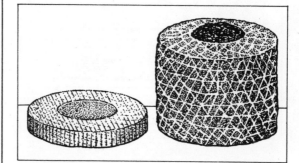

Jiffy-7's cost more, but their mesh construction allows them to be planted directly, as plant roots meet no obstructing wall. Peat pots, in my experience, do not break down as fast as reputed and will hinder small roots.

If a large crop of plants is your aim, then use seed flats made of pressed plant fiber.

When ready to plant your seeds in moss, take the moss and soak it in hot water; cold water takes longer to penetrate the moss fibers. Let it cool, and squeeze out the excess water with your hands. The moss should be wet, but not dripping. Put the pots or flats on waterproof trays and fill to a depth of at least two inches. Tamp the moss down with the palm of your hand, but don't pack it tightly. Now you are ready to sow the seeds.

First read the requirements on the packet. Some seeds must have a period of cold before they will germinate. The process of exposing them to a temperature drop (which works out to be about 40°F.) is called *stratification*; simply store the seeds behind the Jello in the family refrigerator. Stratification is a safety factor built into seeds that grow in a northern climate. It prevents their germination during a January thaw. The instructions will tell you how long to chill the seeds.

If you are worried about how deep to plant the seeds, and the packet doesn't tell you, cover small seeds (one-sixteenth of an inch or larger) by the thickness of one seed. Tiny seeds, like begonias, need not be covered at all. When sowing small seeds, use a folded piece of paper and tap it gently as you move it across the moss.

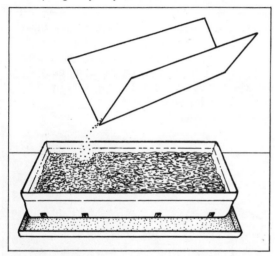

Heating Cables

The single most important reason why many people have trouble with seeds germinating is that the seed bed is too cool. Lack of heat works in combination with the moisture to rot the seeds before they can sprout. The majority of seeds must have warmth for germination to occur, usually between 65°-70°F. The solution is a waterproof, insulated heating cable coupled with a thermostat that is preset to 70°. These are purchased as a complete unit and sold by length. At the time of this writing, a twelve-foot cable capable of heating a growing area of four square feet is under five dollars. Seeds from tropical countries often require even higher temperatures, so should be started in the summer. The only way I ever got a mango to sprout was exposing it to the high temperatures of a compost heap, where it sprouted in October after being thrown out.

Cover your planted containers with plastic wrap or glass, but keep it away from the surface of the moss as drops of moisture will condense (especially when using the cable) and form small swamps that will drown the seeds. This miniature greenhouse will prevent the medium from drying out—an event to be avoided at all costs! Keep the trays near a window, just out of reach of the sun's rays. A lot of sources tell you that complete darkness is necessary for germination but I've never found that to be true. In fact, many seeds need the stimulation of light before they sprout. A few seeds need total darkness, like the forget-me-not and poppy, but the seed packets will tell you.

When the first green shoots appear, move the trays into the direct sunlight (unless you are doing all of this in midsummer), turning them daily to keep the tiny plants from bending to the light. Remove the covering and keep a continual check on the water situation; the moss can dry out very quickly in the heat of the sun. When watering is needed, water directly into the tray until the seedlings are big enough to withstand the weight of water drops.

When the true leaves appear, I transplant to individual peat pots or Jiffy-7's using the standard soil mix. The pointed end of a knife or a plant label makes an excellent tool; just be as gentle as possible. Pick up the plant and lightly cover the roots with soil. It must be reasonably wet, but not mucky. If the plants are still tiny, like begonias, I leave them in their original containers, but thin them out, allowing at least an inch between each. When they are slightly bigger, I thin again leaving only the largest plants.

The seedlings should not be moved into pots until they are at least three inches high.

(A few of the excellent books and government publications on growing plants from seed are listed in the Bibliography.)

ROOTED CUTTINGS

An effortless way to produce new plants is by rooting cuttings. It's faster than raising plants from seed, and the rooted plants have all the characteristics of the mother plant; seeds of many hybrid varieties available today do not always produce offspring with the same appearance as the parents.

If only a few new plants are wanted, I've found the best method is a combination of Jiffy-7's and small plastic food bags. First choose a plant you would like to reproduce, especially if it's a favorite but has become tall and spindly with time. Choose healthy shoots about three to five inches long and cut them off with a sharp knife or razor blade slightly below the point where a leaf joins the stem. Remove any damaged leaves and flowers and neatly slice off a few of the bottom leaves close to the stem. Take an expanded Jiffy pot and make a hole with a pencil or similar object, three-quarters of the pot's depth. Insert the cutting, making sure that the base of the stem touches the bottom of the hole. Firm the soft peat back into place around the stem. Now put the whole affair into a plastic bag with the opening at the top. Unless the air conditions are very dry, you need not seal the bag. In about two weeks, give the cutting a slight tug to check if rooting has commenced. If not, pull out the cutting and check the end for rot. If all looks well, try again, but make doubly sure that the base of the cutting touches the rooting medium; it needs this touch stimulus to start new roots. All this time, make sure that the pot is moist; never let it dry out. When new roots appear, poking through the mesh, plant the Jiffy-7 in a three-inch clay pot.

There are plant hormone products available to induce rooting, but I've never found the additional stimulation necessary, especially if cuttings are started in the spring of the year. When many plants are needed, I use a six-inch clay pot filled with shredded sphagnum moss that is evenly wet, but not soggy, and fairly tightly packed. Cuttings are inserted and the pot placed in a plastic bag. Once again, check on the moisture level of the medium periodically, and if the humidity is extremely low, put a Twistum on the bag. Plastic bags that are sealed should be opened every few days and checked for mold. Stagnant air and damp conditions give mold and fungus a helping hand.

Most tender and herbaceous or non-woody plants may be propagated in this manner and you'll easily add to your plant collection.

Another old-time method is rooting cuttings in a glass of water. It works for ivies, impatiens,

coleus (illustrated), begonias, wandering Jews, geraniums and many more. After the roots begin to grow, add small amounts of sand or soil to the water every day or so, and you will prevent a tangled mass of roots (always the case when pulling them from water) when ready to transplant. You will also have general success as the soil stimulates the growth of root hairs.

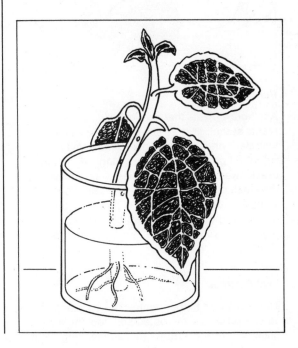

Plants by Division

Another easy way to produce new plants is by division of root stock. Early spring is the best time, before new growth for the season begins. This process works with plants that form multiple crowns like many of the ferns; it's obviously a bad idea with a single-stemmed plant. The chosen plant may be divided into as many sections as there are individual stems or crowns.

Try to separate the roots as carefully as you can, keeping as many as possible attached to their original stem. Many ferns can be split in this manner when they have become potbound. Snake plants, cast iron plants, and others of this type, make excellent subjects.

Runners

Any house plants that produce runners with tiny plants at their tips, as strawberry geraniums (illustrated) and spider plants (*Chlorophytum* Spp.) will produce many new plants if the tips are allowed to root. The easiest way is to anchor the small plantlet to a three-inch pot of soil using a bobby pin or paper clip. Make sure that adequate roots have formed, by giving a slight tug, before you cut the runner from the mother plant.

Leaf Cuttings

There is a limit to the number of new plants that can be produced by rooted cuttings; the mother plant has a finite number of suitable stems. But,

if you are in no great rush and want to reproduce a large number of a particular plant, then leaf cuttings are the answer. Three general methods are employed.

The first is used with *Begonia rex.* A large, healthy leaf is chosen and the petiole shortened to the length shown. The main veins are then cut at vein junctions, using a sharp knife or razor blade. The leaf is then laid on a moist bed of sand or peat moss, top side up. The petiole is stuck into the medium and the leaf held in place with small stones or bobby pins. The pot is covered with plastic and kept out of intense light. In a few weeks, miniature replicas of the parent plant will sprout on the leaf surface.

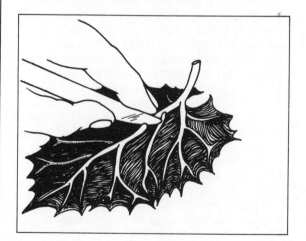

The second method is called leaf-petiole cutting. It's used for Christmas begonias (*Begonia cheimantha*), geraniums, poinsettias, and most other plants with woody or fleshy branches. It's always a good idea to include a part of the stem with a leaf bud present at the point where the petiole meets the stem. Moist sand, peat moss, or vermiculite makes a good rooting medium. The petiole is planted in the medium; make sure that the base rests in the bottom of the hole and the cutting is firmly set. Check for root growth every few weeks and make sure the medium is kept damp. A cluster of growth buds and new roots will be clearly visible at the base of the petiole.

The third method works for thick and succulent leaves like *Crassula*, the cotyledons, and the many sedums. It often happens quite naturally when a leaf falls from a stem and comes to rest on the surface of the soil. If growing conditions are favorable, tiny roots will quickly form. An army of sedums may be manufactured by removing as many leaves as you want, and sticking their bases in a moist rooting medium of sand or peat.

Offshoots

Most bromeliads will bloom only once—the mother plant will die within a few years after flowering. When I first heard this fact from my Florida friend, I was naturally shocked, as it's very rarely mentioned in garden and house-plant books. Then she told me about offshoots, which usually appear around the base of the

mother plant after it has bloomed, and my faith in nature was restored.

The offshoots should not be potted until they are at least eight inches in height and have taken on the characteristics of the mother plant. They should be cut off with a sharp knife as close to the parent as possible and planted in osmunda or other epiphytic media in three-inch pots.

Air-Layering

When a prized dracaena or rubber plant (Ficus) has reached the ceiling, it's time to watch it bend or air-layer it. This is an especially valuable method to produce a mature plant in a short time and relieve the leggy look of rubber plants.

Start the procedure in late spring or early summer by making a diagonal cut, about one and one-half inches long, in the stem at the height you wish the new plant to be. You will have to remove a few leaves above the cut. Keep the cut from healing by inserting a wooden matchstick into the cut. The cut area is then surrounded with thoroughly moistened peat moss or sphagnum and wrapped with plastic, tied top and bottom. Inspect the package every week or

so for signs of new, white roots. When the root system is well developed remove the plastic, but leave the moss and cut the parent stem cleanly, just below the roots. Pot in a five- or six-inch pot and be very gentle as the new roots will be quite brittle.

By removing the top, the remaining stem should start to produce new leaves at the leaf axils along the stem.

Cane Sectioning

Dracaena, Dieffenbachia, and Cordyline may be propagated by cutting their stems into three-inch sections, making sure that each section includes a leaf scar, and then placing them horizontally on a bed of moist sphagnum or peat moss. When rooting is well along, the dormant bud will sprout and a new plant is on the way.

CHAPTER SIX
Lichens, Mosses, and Ferns

In 1829, Dr. Nathaniel Bagshaw Ward, a London botanist, found a moth chrysalis. Wishing to witness the emergence of the adult moth, he enclosed the chrysalis in a glass jar, with soil at the bottom, and closed the top. After a short period of time, he spotted a tiny fern growing in the sealed bottle. The good doctor was delighted, not only because this accident opened up a whole new field of plant research,* but he had found a way to finally grow ferns in the foul air of London.

His invention was called the Wardian Case, and is now termed a terrarium. Poor Dr. Ward must be turning over in his grave these past few years, as banks use his idea as a come-on for new accounts, and Sunday supplement pages promise a "new world of green, that lasts forever in a bottle . . . beauty beyond belief (plants not included)." Department stores now offer ready-made terrariums in narrow-necked bottles for quite fantastic prices, and the craze goes on.

*Dr. Ward continued to refine the original bottle garden, and in time, his idea was used to transport rare and exotic plants across the seas in complete health and safety.

Nevertheless, a good idea much maligned, is still a good idea and fabricating terrariums can be a fascinating occupation.

MAKING A TERRARIUM

Many people enjoy the "ship-in-a-bottle" approach to making terrariums. You take a large bottle, like a demijohn, with the narrowest neck you can find, and by dint of great manual dexterity, and long-handled tools, plant a conversation piece. There are problems: plants grow, change positions, and litter, not to mention pests and diseases.

I prefer glass bowls with sufficient openings that enable me to remove overgrown plants, trim leaves, and remove leaf-litter. The old-fashioned, flat-sided goldfish bowls still available in variety stores are fine too.

First take your chosen container and clean the glass thoroughly; then dry completely to prevent soil from sticking to its sides. Put a mixture of clean stones, gravel and some charcoal chips over the bottom, so that any excess water is held away from the soil. Now cover the stones with a piece of plastic screening (cheap metal screening will rust and decay, while aluminum screening will form an oxide that might not be beneficial to the plants above). Buy or make a water wick, pushing half through a small hole in the screening and spread the rest above. This will absorb any excess water and slowly distribute to the soil above.

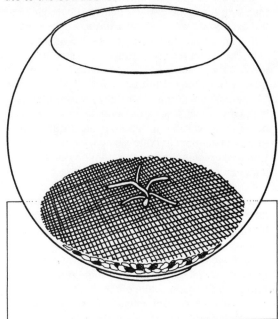

Now add your soil mix made to the following proportions:

1/4 humus or leaf mold
1/4 sphagnum moss
1/4 peat moss
1/4 sand and gravel

As we've mentioned before, use sterilized soil; any mold or mildew spores in unsterilized soil would have a field day in the closed atmosphere of a terrarium.

Slowly spread the soil mix over the wick and screening, making sure that the mix is damp, but not wet. A good rule of thumb is to make the soil and drainage material equal to about one-quarter of the depth of your container.

Now you are ready to plant, spreading the roots out and gently but firmly covering them with soil. Take it slowly to prevent dirtying the clean glass. When planting is finished, carefully water the soil. Any excess will drain to the bottom to be redistributed to the soil by the wick. Obtain a piece of glass for a cover and remove it once a day to allow for air circulation, unless your bowl is planted with bog plants which need high humidity. If too much moisture condenses on the container sides, it's bad for most plants and should be remedied by removing the cover and allowing excess water to evaporate.

Unless you've made a desert terrarium (by following the same general plan, but substituting the cactus-soil mix and following a reduced watering schedule), keep the smaller bowls away from the direct rays of midday sun; temperatures in these containers can rise rapidly and quickly bake the contents.

The best terrarium, especially for wild plants, is the aquarium. It fits well upon a shelf, and covers are available with built-in illumination, allowing placement in otherwise dark corners. Due to its rectangular shape, sections of plantings can be easily changed without disturbing the rest.

A typical one-gallon size measures about 9 by 6 by 7 inches; the four-gallon size is 13 1/2 by 9 1/2 by 9. Larger sizes are available, up to fifty gallons or more.

Remove the glass on one of the long sides by peeling away the flexible aquarium cement and replacing the pane with a piece of mirror. The mirror will reflect light, make the plant display appear larger, and act as a sun shade.

By using individual plants potted in small containers, such as plastic margarine cups, custard cups, thimble-sized clay pots, or larger containers if the plant and aquarium are big enough to warrant it, you can mix many types of plants: Wild flowers that require winter dormant periods may be enjoyed till their leaves fade in fall, and easily removed for the following year. Acid-loving ferns may be grouped with flowering bulbs; small insectivores like the parrot pitcher plant—which enjoys water at the roots—can live in harmony with a small Bird's Nest Fern. The combinations are endless and allow for a great deal of experimentation.

The bottom of the aquarium should have a layer of stones and gravel—about an inch will do—to insure adequate drainage. If you use containers without drainage holes, put some crocking in the bottom before adding soil.

When planting, put the small containers to the front, with the larger pots at the rear, filling the gaps between with sand or gravel or sphagnum moss, and moss-covered rocks to achieve a naturalistic look.

Many wild plants adapt quite readily to terrarium conditions, and this chapter and Chapter 11 mention many of them. The following is a list of popular house plants that will do well, especially when young, at average room temperatures without direct sunlight:

Variegated Chinese evergreen, *Aglaonema commutatum*

Spotted evergreen, *A. costatum*

Queen's tears, *Billbergia nutans*

Dwarf mountain palm, *Chamaedorea elegans*

Miniature grape ivy, *Cissus striata*

Earthstars, *Cryptanthus* spp.

Gold-dust dracaena, *Dracaena godseffiana*

Ribbon plant, *D. sanderiana*

Persian violet, *Exacum affine*

Creeping fig, *Ficus pumila*

Hahn's self-branching ivy, *Hedera helix* 'Hahn's Self-branching'

Bloodleaf, *Iresine herbstii*

Coral-bead plant, *Nertera granadensis*

Artillery plant, *Pilea microphylla*

Satin pothos, *Scindapsus pictus argyraeus*

Wandering Jew, *Tradescantia fluminensis*

Silvery wandering Jew, *Zebrina pendula*

LICHENS

Lichens are a lowly (botanically speaking) form of plant life composed of algae and fungi living together in a partnership called *symbiosis*. Each partner contributes to the welfare of the other—the algae gaining a controlled environment relating to water supply and protection from the elements, and the fungi receiving nutrients from the chlorophyll activities of the algae. It's a strange partnership that is not entirely understood by botanists. When the fungus and its algal partner are separated in the laboratory, no one has ever been able to reunite them and even approximate the original form.

Lichens provide food for small insects and large mammals. In the Arctic, reindeer moss (*Cladonia* spp.) is the principal diet of caribou during winter; in our own northeast, deer often survive by feeding on local tree lichens (*Parmelia* spp.) when no other food is available. In extreme emergencies, hungry explorers have survived on lichen soup.

Litmus paper, known to all chemistry students, is filter paper that has been impregnated with lichen dyes that are blue in basic solutions and turn red in the presence of acid solutions.

In the long run of nature, the greatest service performed by lichens is pioneering the lengthy process of soil formation; they grow where little else is found, and through the centuries, contribute to the build-up of organic matter and eventually become hosts to other small plants such as mosses.

Don't look for lichens in the heavily polluted urban areas, as they are intolerant of sulfur dioxide and other components of "dirty air." A few may be found growing in suburbs, but the majority need the clean, cool air and pure water of country hills and mountains.

Keep them to a minimum in mixed terrariums as they are touchy to establish. In nature, they are usually found in the open with plenty of light and air. When subjected to wet conditions for too long a period, the fungus grows at a much faster rate than the algae, and starves to death. They are well equipped to withstand long periods of drought by going into hibernation until water is once again available.

I always collect lichens when growing on small rocks, pieces of wood, or branches, so the plants are raised above the terrarium floor, preventing them from becoming too wet. They require fresh air, so are not suitable subjects for a completely sealed container.

Lichens generally reproduce by asexual means, simply forming new plants from broken pieces of the old. They also produce fruiting bodies which are the bright patches of color found on top of their tiny branches, that produce spores,* but no one has ever successfully produced new lichens by germinating these spores. The whole matter is further complicated by the knowledge that the fungal spore must find a compatible alga to join it before a lichen is produced.

The illustration shows some of the more common varieties found in America. Individual species are sometimes difficult to identify without chemical testing, so lichenology has the potential of a lifetime hobby.

Be sure to examine them with a hand lens to clearly see the complexity of form and variations in color.

1 British soldiers (*Cladonia cristatella*): Found growing on branches, bark and mosses, and on the ground. They are named after the Redcoats of revolutionary war fame.

2 Reindeer moss (*C. rangiferina*): Found in large clumps, generally on rocks in elevated places.

3 Pink earth lichen (*Baeomyces roseus*): Likes conditions wetter than most, and grows directly on poor soil. The pink fruiting bodies are of such intense color on gray and misty days, they can be spotted yards away.

4 Boulder lichen (*Parmelia conspersa*): Grows on rocks, boulders, and stone walls. They look like mountains on the Moon.

5 Goblet lichen (*Cladonia pyxidata*): Found among mosses on the southeastern side of barren hills. A goblet lichen looks exactly like its popular name.

*Spores are reproductive bodies formed by algae. lichens. fungi, mosses, and ferns. They usually contain but one cell and are only one of many steps that lead to a new plant. Seeds are produced only by conifers and flowering plants and contain an actual embryo plant of many different cells and a complicated structure. Seeds grow directly into adults upon germination.

X 3/4

MOSSES

Mosses are familiar plants of shady habitat. Some are aquatic; many grow in soil or on rocks; the bark of trees, living and dead; stone walls; broken sidewalks; brick buildings and shingled roofs. Although generally classed with liverworts, they differ in having a midrib on the leaf and a tolerance for dryer surroundings.

The leafy growth of mosses are really branches that arise from a spreading green filament produced by a germinating spore. This green filament or protonema grows above and below the soil surface (or anything it can cling to) and when mature, produces the branches and tiny roots or rhizoids. Rhizoids do not grow deeply, just deep enough to hold the plant and absorb water, making mosses very easy to transplant.

When a moss reaches maturity, male and female sex organs are produced on the tops of the leafy shoots. At the time of fertilization these organs swell with water, releasing male sperm cells. With larger mosses, the sperm travel to adjacent eggs when splashed by falling rain. Smaller species depend on dew or melting snow and the sperm swim to the egg. The resulting embryo, or *sporophyte*, develops into a long stalk with a foot that buries itself in the leaves of the moss absorbing minerals and water. The upper end forms a capsule filled with tiny spores. The sporophyte has its own chloroplasts

and manufactures food but is still a parasite on the plants below. When the capsule matures, chloroplasts fade, the sporophyte turning a rich brown color. Now the capsule looses its top and reveals a circle of teeth, that control the release

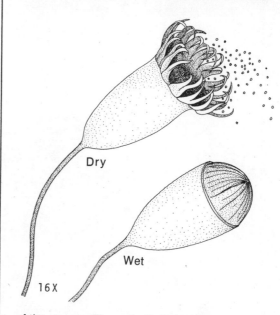

Dry

Wet

16 X

of the spores. These teeth are sensitive to humidity and when the air is damp, they remain closed, but when air is dry, they open. The spores are shaken into the wind by a miniature saltcellar.

Liverwort
Marchantia polymorpha

X 1

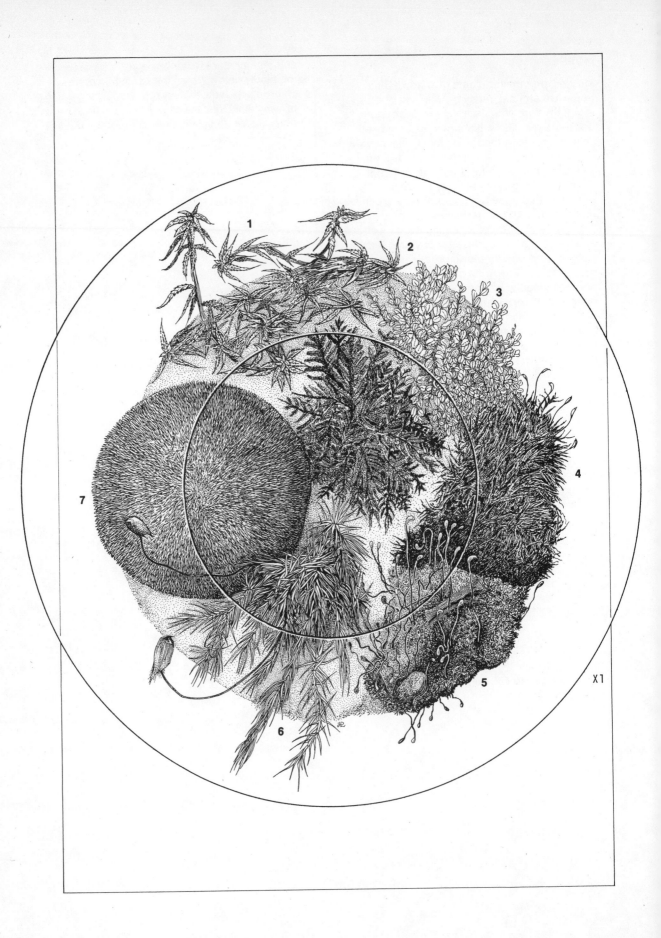

Most mosses prefer shade. Since they have a poorly developed water distribution system, hot sun dries them out before the water can reach the thirsty cells. The hair-cap moss (*Polytrichum commune*) our largest and most common moss, will grow in open fields, but grass provides some shade and the dew of morning furnishes needed water. Mosses are usually subject to rapid changes of moisture and have developed the ability to "fold-up" their leaves when dry, markedly changing their appearance, as they look dehydrated.

When collecting mosses for a home terrarium, take a pH tape along and check the acidity of the local soil. Most mosses are finicky about pH and will quickly die if the balance is not maintained.

The illustration shows seven common mosses of the United States.

1 Sphagnum moss (*Sphagnum acutifolium*) is the common species found in wet and boggy places. As sphagnum matures, the older parts of the plant begin to decay, while the younger moss continues to grow on the top. The decayed sphagnum is called peat moss and over a period of years it will slowly encircle and fill small ponds, turning them into quagmire.

2 Feather moss (*Hypnum crista-castrensis*) forms dense masses of yellow-green, plume-like branches and is one of our most beautiful mosses. Look for it on rich woodsy soil, under the shade of trees.

3 Woodsy mnium (*Mnium cuspidatum*) is common in parks, lawns, and moist woods where it grows on soil or decayed wood. When dry, it quickly shrinks and the tiny leaves look like wrinkled tissue paper. When water is again abundant, the leaves become a bright glossy green. One of the first sights of spring are the green sporophytes.

4 Fern moss (*Thuidium delicatulum*) grows in dense mats on earth, stones, and dead tree branches, and looks much like fine embroidery done with a lustrous, dark-green thread.

5 Cord moss (*Funaria hygrometrica*) has capsule stalks that are straight when wet and twisted like rope when dry. Reacting to minute changes in humidity, this coiling action lends itself to an overall spore distribution. Look for it on old, abandoned foundations and burned-over soil.

6 Hair-cap moss (*Polytrichum commune*) grows stems up to a foot long. The sporophytes appear in early spring or late autumn, maturing in July. Considered a weed by most farmers, it was once used by early Americans to stuff pillows.

7 Pincushion moss (*Leucobryum glaucum*) forms large gray-white tufts found in moist woods, looking exactly like its common name. If introduced to a terrarium, they often give a bonus of seedlings from nearby flowering plants.

Meadow Spike moss

In addition to mosses, a tiny, pale-green creeping plant belonging to the Selaginellas or spike mosses, grows in Northeastern America. Found in meadows, along ponds and streams, and sometimes lawns, it's an excellent little plant for a woodsy terrarium. The leaves are evergreen when given the protection of a terrarium.

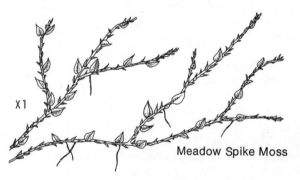

X 1

Meadow Spike Moss

FERNS

Two hundred fifty million years ago, vast jungles of tree-sized club mosses, horsetails and ferns covered much of the earth. The giant aspects of these plants has vanished with time, but when walking through a shady woods in midsummer surrounded by the lacy growth of ferns, the jungle effect can be readily appreciated.

Ferns do not bear flowers but reproduce with spores produced on the leaves. Their stem, called a rhizome, either creeps along the ground year by year or stays in one place forming a central crown which slowly increases in size. The rhizomes are perennial. The leaves in many of the northern species die down every fall and are deciduous in character. Others are evergreen as most of the tropical species. Roots are adventitious and grow from the lower side of the rhizomes.

Ferns are relatively easy to transplant, but make sure the soil conditions of the wild match those of cultivation. They are easily divided by cutting the rhizomes. As with most plants, spring is the best time to do this. Dividing ferns with crowns is a bit more tricky; cut the crown with a sharp knife, trying not to disturb the foliage and roots.

Life Cycle of a Fern

Ferns begin their life cycle by producing spores that are discharged from clusters of spore cases called *sori.* Sori are found on the undersides of fern leaves and are often mistaken for insect infestation or disease. A few ferns like osmunda (*Osmunda* spp.) and sensitive fern (*Onoclea sensibilis*) send up special stalks bearing spore cases which are easily recognized because they lack leaves, but they are in a distinct minority.

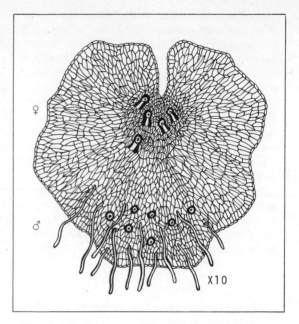

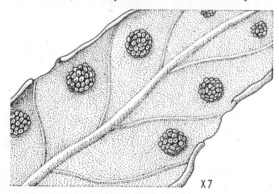

The spore cases, at first green, turn brown as they mature. When dry, the walls of the sori bend back and discharge the dustlike spores to the air. Just as with mosses, when humidity is high, the sori walls stay closed.

With proper conditions of temperature and moisture, the spores germinate and grow into a flat, heart-shaped structure about one-quarter-of-an-inch wide, called a *prothallium.* Separate male and female organs grow on the underside and produce eggs and sperms. With water from dew, rain, or snow as a medium, the sperm swim to the egg and fertilize it. In a short time an embryo fern begins to develop.

Propagating Ferns

Although the fern life cycle sounds a bit complex, they are very easy to grow from spores. Unlike flowering plants, all fern species have the same general requirements for germination.

Absolutely sterile conditions are mandatory. The growing conditions for fern spores match those of mold, fungi, and other undesirables. Use three-inch clay pots, scrubbed and clean, or a Riviera self-watering pot. I favor the Riviera because it keeps the medium moist without constant watching and still allows air circulation from the pot bottom.

Crock the clay pots, and fill to one-inch of the rim with a sterilized soil mix of one-third potting soil, one-third peat moss, and one-third sand. Tamp the mix, making it smooth and level. Soak the clay pots and drain excess water.

Cast the spores at any time of the year, one species to a pot, using the folded paper method from the seed germination chapter. Cover the pots with glass and put them in a warm spot (65°F.-70°F.), away from direct sunlight. Check the medium to keep it from drying out. If it starts to dry, soak the pots, don't water from the top. The germinating spores should not be disturbed.

Some species will germinate within a few days, others will take a few weeks, so be patient. As the prothallia grows, a green cast will appear on the surface of the soil. In about three months time, the prothallia will reach its full three-quarter-inch size. If you have achieved excellent spore germination, thin the prothallia out so they are about an inch apart. One of the interesting things I remember from college botany is that only the male organs will usually develop if the prothalli are too close together, so I always thin them out at this stage. Falling condensation from the glass cover should provide enough water for the sperm to swim to the egg, but you might have to mist the surface. The tiny plants will now begin to develop. As the leaves grow larger you will have to thin the plants again. When three or more fronds have appeared, transplant to individual pots. You will now have a more-than-adequate supply of native (or tropical) ferns for your terrarium where they should thrive until large enough to go outdoors.

When growing ferns in pots or in terrariums it is not at all unlikely for germination to take place entirely without your help or knowledge, and baby ferns will pop up in the most unlikely places. I have a mango tree in a self-watering pot, and last year noticed that the soil was covered with green—I immediately thought of an algae attack until I examined the growth under a microscope and found prothalli from spores of a fan table fern (*Pteris cretica* 'Wilsonii') located about five pots away.

Collecting Native Ferns

When collecting native ferns (or any other plant) remember that you are gathering plants and not out to lay waste to field and woods. Don't dig any plants on state and public lands, as they are usually protected by law. If collecting in a woods that is not your own, ask permission from the owners. You'll be surprised by the generosity of most landowners, if you're polite enough to ask. Land slated for imminent destruction by developers is a good place to look for plants, because they'll be destroyed if not removed, but make an attempt at getting permission anyway, so your conscience is clear. And don't overlook roadside ditches out in the country, as many ferns enjoy the moist conditions found there.

Tender or Hardy Ferns

Ferns are tender or hardy, and evergreen or deciduous depending on their environment and type. The tropical and southern ferns are tender and will not survive northern winters outside. Our northern ferns are perennials and hardy. Some drop their leaves every autumn and many are evergreen. I've grown hardy, deciduous ferns indoors that have been brought into the house when mature. They must have a dormant period during the winter, and unless you have a greenhouse, they prefer terrarium conditions

while in active growth. The evergreens, although green during the winter demand the same rest period. If you have ample storage space, about 40°-45°F., these ferns make wonderful pot plants for summer decoration, then stored till the following year.

So when collecting live plants, wait till the end of the growing season, before the first frost in your area. Choose young and small plants. Deciduous ferns, if very young, will stay green all winter under terrarium conditions. Dig deeply enough to protect the rhizomes and take enough soil to keep the plants from wilting on the way home. Put your specimens in plastic bags, but don't seal the tops. Always make a note of the locality where you found them for future trips and test the pH of the soil. A lot of ferns are not fussy about pH, but a few resent any change.

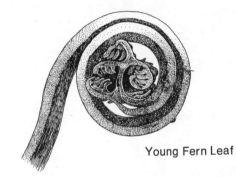

Young Fern Leaf

Collecting Spores

Most ferns have mature sori in the early fall, and in my opinion the best way of getting plants is to grow your own. When asked, most gardeners and growers do not mind giving a tiny section of leaf to an interested person. Ferns usually suffer some damage to their leaves during the summer by animals and weather, so it's no problem finding broken leaves to take home without disturbing established plants.

The illustration shows three hardy evergreen native American ferns suitable for terrariums:

1 Ebony spleenwort (*Asplenium platyneuron*) is an evergreen found from Maine to Florida. It grows from nine to eighteen inches high, with dark-green shining leaves. While said to prefer alkaline soil, I have two growing beautifully under a large white pine and surrounded by pine needles, so keep your eyes open wherever you are!

2 Common polypody (*Polypodium vulgare*) generally grows about six inches high and is evergreen. *Vulgare* is the Latin word for common when used with plants, for this fern is not vulgar in any sense. In nature it prefers to grow on rocks with a minimum of soil throughout North America.

3 Christmas fern (*Polystichum acrostichoides*) is green at Christmas. It varies between a foot or two in height depending on growing conditions, preferring a slightly alkaline soil. Found on rocky, shaded slopes, or around old stone walls from southern Canada to Florida.

X 1/4

TROPICAL FERNS

Unless working with terrariums, the best ferns for the house come from tropical regions of the world. Like their northern cousins, they prefer partial shade during the summer months but winter sunlight is beneficial. Soil should be evenly moist, not wet. The delicate roots need constant water but will not survive in soggy soil. I use the standard potting mix but add another part of sand.

When transplanting, increase the size of pots by one inch, no more. If the fern is a specimen* and the pot is too large already, trim back the roots, repot and thin the foliage to compensate for root loss.

Ferns prefer high humidity so if your rooms are dry, mist the leaves daily, and in summer twice a day.

Average home temperatures will suit most ferns.

If ferns are attacked by scale, and you don't become aware of it until the petioles are covered with these blasted insects, it's best to destroy the plant. Unless the plant is small, it's almost an impossibility to track them all down, and most commercial sprays are harmful to ferns.

The illustration shows four tropical ferns:

1 Crisped blue fern (*Polypodium aureum* 'Mandaianum') grows twelve to eighteen inches high and the leaves are a beautiful milky-blue. To propagate, cut the rhizome.

2 Button fern (*Pellaea rotundifolia*) has fronds to a foot in length. The leaves are dark-green and leathery in appearance. Propagate from spores.

3 Fan maidenhair (*Adenium tenerum* 'Wrightii') has fan-shaped leaflets of a fresh-green color. This fern requires abundant water, so I pot in a self-watering pot. Keep the humidity high, mist often. It likes a rest period in the winter. Divide older plants.

4 Bird's-nest fern (*Asplenium nidus*) sends stiff fronds of shining green from one to three feet in the air, depending on conditions of growth. The new fronds arising from the central crown look like a bird's nest. It too needs abundant moisture and misting and is potted in a self-watering pot. Propagate from spores.

*A specimen plant is usually a perfectly grown and superb example of its species—excellent in every aspect.

X 3/4

X1/2

4

HORSETAILS

Horsetails are represented by one genus, *Equisetum*, and are found throughout North America. The stems have a very high silica content and in pioneer days were used to clean and polish cooking utensils. If you're ever caught on a camping trip without a scouring pad, they really work.

E. hyemale grows along streams, lakes, swamps, in roadside ditches, and often on the edge of railroad beds. The evergreen shoots grow from a perennial rhizome. Since they are not fussy as to drainage, I keep a large clump in a nine-inch pot without a drainage hole. All summer, the pot sits in the full sun and is brought inside in early fall to the sunporch. When outside, rainwater is all it needs, but indoors I water every two weeks or so. Standard potting mix works well, and the clumps are easily divided in spring, when they begin to break the pot.

The spores are in the cone-like caps, and follow the reproductive pattern of ferns. The rings on the shoots have whorls of tiny, scale-like leaves, and photosynthesis occurs primarily in the stem.

The plant grows about three feet tall and has a striking, architectural beauty all its own.

X 3/4

Common Horsetail
Equisetum hyemale

CHAPTER SEVEN
Vines About the Window

Whether fast-flowering or slow-growing, vines are a wonderful addition to the plant types available to the indoor (and terrace) gardener. With free-ranging imagination and a minimum of expense, walls or windows are easily framed with luxuriant growth. The vines pictured in this chapter have few cultural demands, the only real problem being the amount of time you wish to devote making devices that will hold them up!

The following illustration shows a few of the gadgets on the market for fastening strings and fishline to walls of wood, stone, or brick. (See Chapter 16: "Sources of Supply")

1 The Wayward Vine Support consists of small cement disks, about three-quarters of an inch wide, that are glued to brick, stone, tile, or concrete walls. The wire bends easily to hold the vine stem. Supports come in three colors: white, stone gray, and brick red.

2 Feathertown Garden Wall Ties are small plastic disks threaded with green plastic ties. They, too, are affixed to wall surfaces with glue.

3 The Francis Wall Nail is an English import that is worth buying for the box alone. The nails are

steel and should be sharply tapped into the masonry between bricks and concrete blocks. The soft lead strap bends easily to hold where you want it.

4 Canvas picture hooks are glued to plaster walls, making an excellent anchorage for fish line or string.

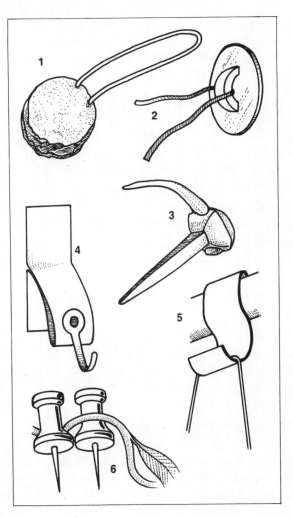

5 Molding hooks are made for hanging mirrors and pictures but do double duty for vines.

6 Map pins, when used in pairs, hold vine stems, especially around doors and fancy woodwork.

In addition, all the basic stock of hardware stores—nails, staples, cuphooks, tile hooks for bathroom walls (not to mention towel bars installed vertically)—can serve the purpose of supporting vines.

In most garden stores, you can buy ready-made, folding trellises of wood which expand to twelve feet in length. Held by a one-by-three inch frame they make a perfect room divider. Or simply make your own with wooden lathing and small aluminum nails.

Even snow-fencing, when stained and attached to a wooden frame, becomes an attractive trellis for vines. Plastic fish line or rope can be strung on a one-by-three inch frame from cup hooks to screen a public window effectively. If you have an electric drill, use evenly spaced holes to replace the hooks.

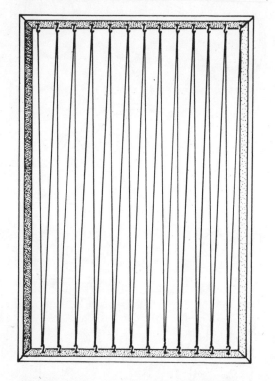

Another very effective support for a large vine such as a passion flower can be made from aluminum clothesline, and a center pole of either doweling or a one-by-one inch piece of wood, cup hooks, and wire. The wire frame can be bent in proportion to the size of the pot used. The center pole should be painted where it is surrounded by soil. Do not use creasote, as this wood preservative is toxic to plant life. Make a movable base of plywood on furniture casters, so the planted pot can be easily moved. The beauty of this design is the amount of vine footage achieved in a limited space.

Or buy a ready-made redwood window box. Put one-by-two inch uprights on either end, drill holes for a piece of doweling, and string fish line from staples or cup hooks over the doweling. Mount on casters for easy movement.

If you don't approve of the handyman image, all the larger garden centers carry outdoor trellises that are easily adapted to indoor use. Use your imagination; vines are not particular and will grow on just about anything.

PASSION FLOWER

In the early 1600's, a unique and exotic flower was discovered in Mexico by a Catholic friar. Because the elaborate floral parts suggested the Passion of Christ in symbolic terms and because it was found in heathen territory, the flower became a *cause célèbre.* The Church interpreted the find as a message from the Lord asking that the natives be converted to Christianity. Of course the natives already used the plant in folk medicine and as an aphrodisiac, attaching a somewhat different meaning to the plant's new name.

The ten petals represent the Apostles, without Peter and Judas; the filiments of the corona are either the Crown of Thorns or a halo; the five anthers are the wounds; the styles are three nails; the three sepals on the floral stem are the Trinity; and the whips of persecution are seen in the coiling tendrils of the vine.

Passiflora caerulea is the Latin name for the original passion flower. Its petals are greenish-white and the rays of the corona are banded with blue and purple.

P. edulis has smaller flowers of white with a purple-banded corona. It bears edible fruit that is grown for market in many places throughout the world. The flowers must be hand pollinated unless the plant is outdoors for the summer.

When growing from seed (a very easy process) sow fresh seed in the spring. Germination takes up to a month, and older seed takes much longer. Use a heating cable to provide adequate warmth. If you are interested in growing the plant for fruit, keep a couple of seedlings, as the quality of the fruit varies greatly from plant to plant.

Passion flowers should have as much sun as possible to guarantee flowers, and with luck a new vine will flower in the second year. Mine grows on a wooden trellis fastened directly to the pot, so the whole affair can be moved outside for the summer.

Temperatures should be above 55°F., though mine has lived through 45°F. without ill effects. Plants cannot abide the shock of sudden changes in temperature, but most of them, with the exception of the truly tropical varieties, can take an occasional slow chill.

Plants will grow in a seven-inch pot for a few years but should be fertilized every three weeks in summer. As the vines increase in size, move on to larger pots using the standard soil mix.

Flowers develop on new growth, so prune the vine once a year while it is dormant. I generally cut back in January, taking about one-third off the canes, and stopping just before a lateral bud.

Once you have a mature plant, you can easily propagate new plants from stem cuttings in the summer months.

Passion Flower
Passiflora edulis

X1

Marble Vine

Bryonopsis laciniosa

X3/4

MARBLE VINE

Marble vine (*Bryonopsis laciniosa*), a member of the gourd family, is a fast-growing annual. In days gone by it was an old favorite on screen porches, the leaves providing shade and the cream-striped marble-sized fruit making a decorative addition. Like all gourds, it needs full sun and bi-monthly feeding. Use the standard soil mix. The plant pictured is in a six-inch pot. The half-inch dowel holds fish-line leads with a staple.

When the vine becomes too leggy, toss it out and start a new one from seed. Never bemoan the fate of an annual plant. Once it flowers, it's done its job.

CLEMATIS

Clematis are woody, perennial vines that climb by twisting their leaf petioles around any handy support and produce magnificent flowers of white, pink, blue, purple and all shades in between. The petals are really brightly colored sepals and not true petals at all.

There are two main types: those that flower from new growth each year and are usually hardy enough to endure northern winters, and species that flower on old wood, year after year. Generally the types that flower on new wood are sold in northern garden centers. It's important to know, because of the potential danger in pruning old-wood bloomers.

Buy a two-year-old plant from a nursery. (Growing from seed is a lengthy process, since germination may take a year or more.) Pot in a five-inch pot and add a tablespoon of lime to the standard soil mix. This is important, since clematis do poorly in acid soil. Your purchased plant will usually have a small plastic trellis or a stake to support the stem. Remove it and replace with three-foot stakes. Be very careful; the stem is extremely brittle and very easy to snap. Keep the soil evenly moist and place in a sunny window with daytime temperatures never above 60°F. If you cannot keep the sun away from the roots, mulch them with some vermiculite or perlite; clematis roots must be kept cool. They stay near the surface of the soil and not only resent acid soil but heat as well. Don't mulch with peat moss, since it is acid.

You will be rewarded for your care with a startling display of flowers which bloom from late fall to spring. When blooming ceases, cut the stems back to about two feet and store it in a cool place for the summer, keeping the soil

Clematis
Clematis lanuginosa 'Belle Nantaise'

×¾

X 3/4

Cardinal Climber
Quamoclit sloteri

Cypress Vine
Q. pennata

Flag of Spain
Q. lobata

moist enough to prevent drying out the plant. When summer ends, bring in the pot and start the flowers again. Fertilize once a month starting the second year.

The illustration is *Clematis languinosa* 'Belle Nantaise' and is a lovely shade of blue.

QUAMOCLIT

Three easily grown members of the morning-glory family, cardinal climber (*Quamoclit sloteri*), cypress vine (*Q. pennata*), and the flag of Spain (*Q. lobata*) are perfect for brightening up a dull winter afternoon with their bright and cheerful flowers and fresh green foliage.

Seeds germinate easily if soaked overnight in warm water, as the seed coats are very tough. Plant the seedlings in four- or five-inch pots any time of year and place in a sunny and warm window. Use the standard mix and keep evenly moist. They'll generally flower within ten weeks.

Use plenty of string or fish line. The Flag of Spain can easily reach fifteen feet indoors, if conditions are to its liking.

Cardinal climber is bright red; cypress vine has white flowers; and flag of Spain has red buds which slowly turn to lemon yellow as they mature. I mean slowly, as it takes several weeks for these buds to open.

The lines in the illustration are held by canvas picture hooks, a boon for the apartment-dwellers whose landlords hate anything that mars plaster.

I haven't pictured the common morning glory (*Ipomoea* spp.) but remember that it grows easily indoors following the same cultural directions as above. When vines become leggy, toss them out and start anew.

GLORIOSA

Gloriosa (*Gloriosa rothschildiana*) is called the climbing lily: the plant bends its leaf tips to support the weak stem and thus can climb to as high as six feet. Gloriosa is also called the glory lily, an obvious title once you see the beautiful lily-like flowers with bright red petals that turn to yellowish-orange at the floral base.

The plants grow from tubers, and by alternating plantings, you can have them blooming throughout the year. They need at least four hours of sun to bloom and night temperatures should not go below 60°F. They will survive cooler temperatures for short periods, but resent it. Use the standard potting mix. The soil should not be soggy; allow it to dry slightly between waterings.

Plant the tubers in January for summer bloom and in the fall for winter bloom. Cover with soil about the thickness of one tuber. The purple "eyes" are easily broken, so use care. After the flowers fade, withhold moisture and allow the tubers to dry and rest. Propagate by dividing the tubers or by offsets (the baby tubers produced by the mother tuber).

Occasionally one finds other species for sale in out-of-the-way catalogs. They all require the same treatment.

Put one flower in a small glass vase, and wait for the compliments to begin.

GRAPE IVY

Most vines require sunlight to succeed, but grape ivies (*Cissus* spp.) like filtered sunlight or the equivalent of about 1500 FC. They will tolerate 500 FC but show a definite slowdown in growth rate.

The common grape ivy (*Cissus rhombifolia*) is a willing rambler with fresh green leaves, brownish undersides and hairy brown stems.

Keep them at a temperature above 60°F. and pot them in the standard mix, maintaining evenly moist conditions. Put up plenty of line for climbing.

The illustration shows a commercially manufactured Wessenden Instant Trellis, made of kiln-dried European whitewood with aluminum nails. This trellis is a godsend for the person who hates tools. It can be easily fastened to walls with cup hooks. I made a simple frame of one-by-twos and hooked it to a plaster wall with molly screws from the local hardware store.

This ivy is doing very well (over one year) in a self-watering pot and a soil-less growing mix of straight vermiculite. One-half strength liquid plant food is applied to the water once a month and the vine is pinched occasionally to hold its shape. If you need a fast, easy solution to a drab corner this is it.

Other members of the cissus family are:

Kangaroo vine (*C. antarctica*) tolerates warm temperatures but would do better at an average of 55°F. If you have an air conditioner try this vine. The leaves are a bright green with brown veining.

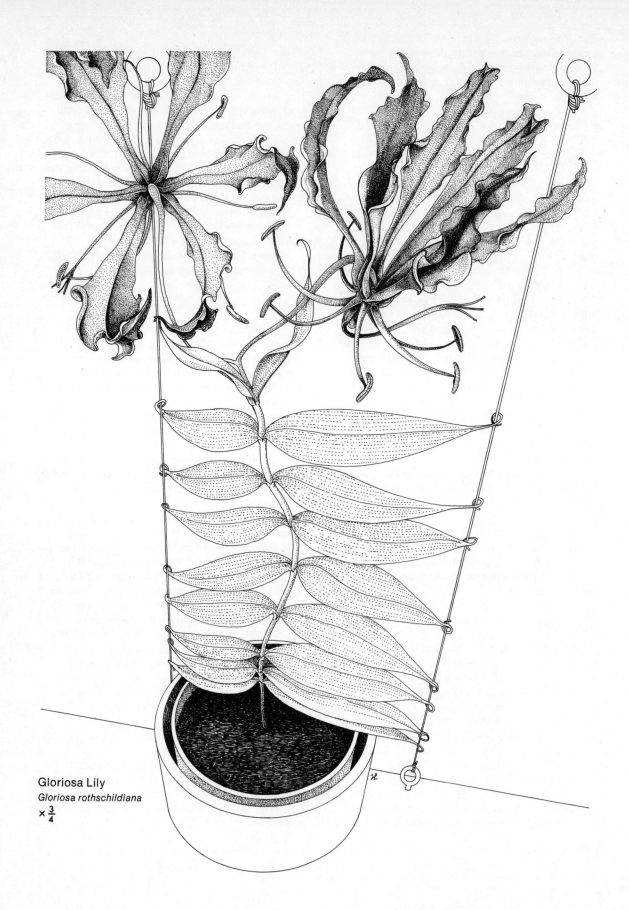

Gloriosa Lily
Gloriosa rothschildiana
$\times \frac{3}{4}$

Rex begonia vine (*C. discolor*) has beautiful leaves with silvery edges and purple velvet centers. It needs warmth—cold air sends it into immediate dormancy. Give it a daily misting, as this plant thrives on humidity.

Miniature grape ivy (*C. striata*) is a little plant with one-and-one-half inch leaves of a medium green color with reddish undersides.

HEARTLEAF PHILODENDRON

A few words about America's most maligned plant, the heartleaf philodendron (*Philodendron oxycardium*). Whether received as a get-well present or purchased at the supermarket, this plant is immediately shoved into a dark corner where, in spite of constant neglect, it hangs on and even grows a few two-inch leaves. But— give it good light (400 FC) high temperatures (60° F. at night and up to 75° or 85°F. during the day) and, most important, a trellis, and you'll be amazed at its upward progress and the new leaves of six inches or more. This plant is a climber, using aerial roots for support; once given an opportunity it goes to town. Stick it in a bronzed baby shoe and it does nothing.

Pot philodendron in the standard mix and keep it evenly moist. When aerial roots develop, the pot assumes the status of an unused home; keep the soil moist, but now start to mist the leaves and roots daily. Twice a month apply a half-strength liquid fertilizer directly to the leaves with a misting can. This is called foliar feeding, and it was quite a surprise to botanists

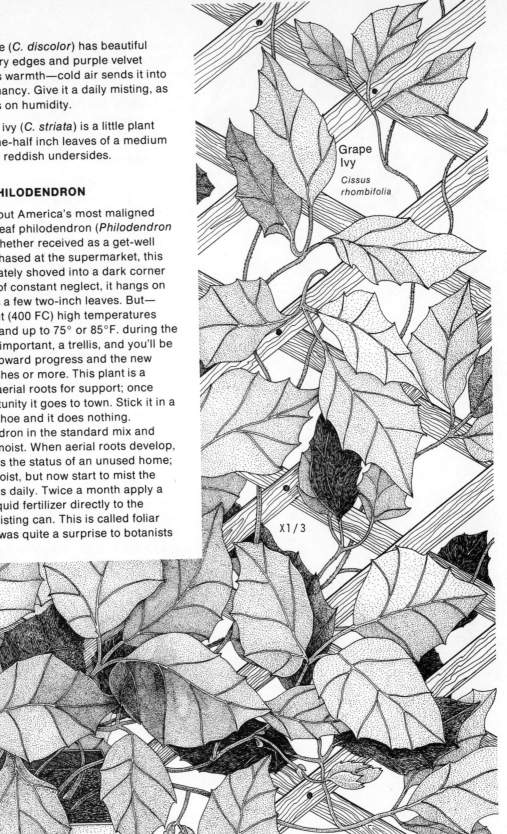

Grape Ivy

Cissus rhombifolia

X1/3

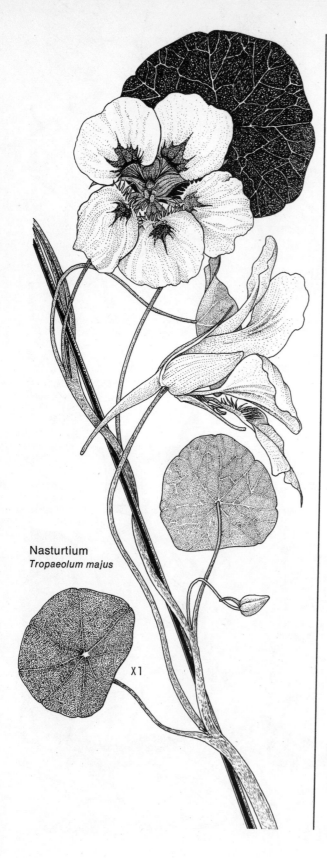

Nasturtium
Tropaeolum majus

X1

when they found that many plants can absorb food directly in this fashion.

Following these steps, you'll have a jungle in no time.

Heartleaf philodendron propagates easily by rooted cuttings.

NASTURTIUM

Grandmother's favorite for flowers and salads, it becomes a charming and inexpensive flowering vine for the sunny winter window.

Climbing nasturtium (*Tropaeolum majus*) requires at least four hours of sun to flower, and also cool temperatures—45°-55°F. at night and up to 70°F. during the day. Soil is the standard mix, but cut down on the composted manure and add more sand. These plants do well in poor soils. Keep evenly moist. By sowing seeds in late summer you'll have winter bloom.

Flowers come in yellow, orange or red and have a delightful perfume.

These plants climb by twisting the leaf petioles around a support and should be placed near a window. If not, the leaves stretch to reach the light and get very leggy. Fertilize once a month. This plant is an annual and will only last through the winter.

TUBER NASTURTIUM

The tuber nasturtium (*T. tuberosum*) is a perennial member of the family with five-lobed leaves and golden-yellow flowers. It readily climbs to about eight feet. Plant the tubers about two inches deep, three to a five-inch pot, using the soil suggested for climbing nasturtiums.

It's important to keep the soil evenly moist but not soggy, or the tubers will rot. In addition, they prefer filtered sunlight during midday hours.

After flowering, the tubers require a rest, but leave them in the pot and just withhold water. I've never attempted to grow these plants in winter, but it's worth a try.

ASPARAGUS FERN

Called bride's bouquet or asparagus fern (*Asparagus plumosis*) this plant is not to be confused with *A. sprengeri*, another member of the clan with the same common name. Bride's bouquet is often used for "ferns" in floral arrangements because of its delicate, lacy fronds. A mature plant (two or three years) will produce stems up to two feet in length, gracefully arching from the pot and taking plenty of room. The stems have small green thorns and in midwinter tiny starlike blossoms appear within the needle-like leaves.

When the plant is a few years old, the stems get longer and start to twist about in search of something to climb, and they'll search every-where. My plant sat in a self-watering pot unat-tended for two weeks and completely entwined a lamp three feet away.

Use the standard soil mix and fertilize three or four times a year. If planted in a clay pot, let the soil dry slightly between waterings. Asparagus ferns like cool temperatures at night, between 50° and 55°F., with a daytime average of 70°F. They will tolerate 45°F. They prefer partial shade; midday summer sun can burn the tiny leaves.

Propagate with seeds or by dividing the crown.

GOURDS

Decorative gourd plants do extremely well in-doors if you give them the environment that the whole squash family requires: lots of sun, plenty of warmth, evenly moist soil and bimonthly feed-ings of plant food. They also need a large win-dow, for these vines should grow to eight feet before you prune them. Since the female flowers produce the fruit and grow only on lateral branches, while the male flowers grow from the main stem, you must pinch back the vine. Its natural inclination is to keep growing straight, branching only once or twice and producing very little fruit. When you pinch the terminal end it forces many branches; if each of these are pinched, more side branches are produced, and believe me when I say you need a large window. Pollenate the female flowers unless you are growing these vines outside.

Even if you are not interested in the fruit, the vines are very attractive and the big yellow flow-ers quite a showpiece, although they only last a day.

The gourds are ready to pick when the stem shrivels and dries out. When the vine becomes spent-looking or too straggly, throw it out and start another.

CUP-AND-SAUCER VINE

Rosy-purple two-inch flowers sit on a green, saucer-shaped calyx resembling a cup in a saucer. This perennial vine germinates in fifteen days in any season and is such a rampant climber that's it's usually regarded as an annual.

Use the standard potting mix, keeping the soil evenly moist, and if growing as a perennial, start to fertilize once a month after the plant is a year old. A 60°F. average temperature suits it but it needs at least four hours of sun daily to flower.

Allow a resting period during winter, reducing water. You can shear it back at this time, and you'll probably have to. Or hack it down and start a new one from seed or rooted cuttings. If the vine flowers during the winter months, then allow it a rest during summer.

The Latin name is *Cobea scandens*. A white variety is known as *C. scandens alba*.

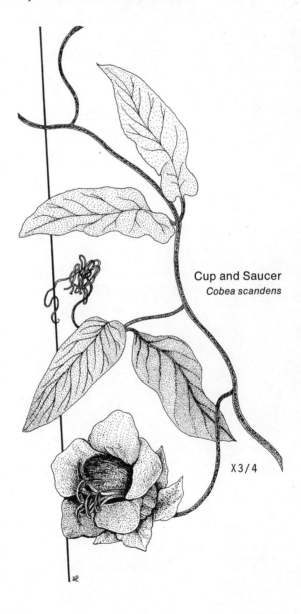

Cup and Saucer
Cobea scandens

X3/4

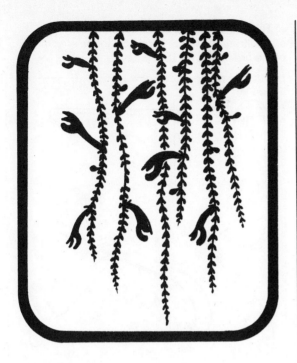

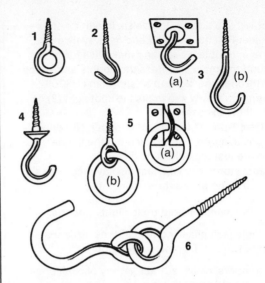

CHAPTER EIGHT
Hanging Gardens

The more time one devotes to growing plants the more plants invade the home. They soon cover all available tables and shelves, take all niches, all corners, and with the addition of lights, take over available closets, the cellar and even the attic. There is only one way to go and that's up to the ceiling. This chapter describes how to get the plants up there, what to put them in, and a selection of varieties that seem especially suitable to such display.

Almost any plant can be planted in a hanging pot, and some of the plants shown here would do equally well in a table or shelf container, but their flowers or leaves look their best when spilling over the edge of a pot, reaching for the floor.

HANGING HARDWARE

The following illustration shows some of the items that may be used to hook a pot to the ceiling or window frame. Be sure to pick a size in proportion to the weight. A pot that contains a plant and dirt can get quite heavy, and with water added would be a formidable task for a small hook. Always use the ceiling beams or top of window frames, and don't depend on plaster board or plaster to hold any weight.

1 Screw eyes: available from 1/2-inch to 3 7/8-inches long.

2 Round-end screw eyes: 1/2-inch to 3 7/8-inches and even larger.

3 Clothesline hooks: (a) square plate design is screwed to the beam; (b) regular hook is screwed into the beam.

4 Cup hooks: from 1/2-inch to 1 1/2-inch.

5 Hitching rings: (a) square plate; (b) lag thread. Both have 2-inch rings.

6 Hammock hook: for the ultimate plant. The hook and eye are four inches long.

To get the pot to the hook, use rope, nylon cord, chain, or monofilament fishing line. The illustration attempts to improve my written description of a double-clinch knot. (Just a regular

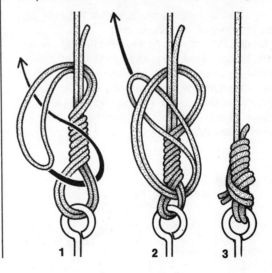

knot will slip apart.) Double six to eight inches of the line. Pull the doubled end halfway through the eye; double it back and make five turns around the main line. Pass the double end of the line through the big loop as shown in (1). Pull the end up slowly and make the knot tight (2). Cut off the excess line (3).

Use 50-pound test line or stronger. Not only are you assured of its holding but the thinner lines are just too difficult to tie.

Most stores have a chain display these days. The following shows three to look for:

1 Sash chain: will hold up to eighty pounds.

2 Single jack chain: comes in three sizes that hold ten, sixteen, or forty-three pounds.

3 Plumbers' chain: a brass variety of sash chain that will hold thirty-five pounds.

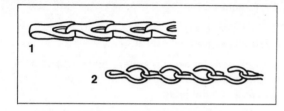

Try to avoid swag chains. They are cheaply made, will hold little weight, and the finish quickly fades.

To get the chain to the ceiling hook use S-hooks:

They come in a variety of sizes from 1/2-inch up and are finished in brass or zinc.

Since plants always turn toward the light and must be occasionally revolved to keep from growing lopsided, take advantage of an old fishing tackle item: the brass snap swivel. I use size 3/0, as it holds most everything and looks decorative as well. Just turn the hanging pots without effort every few days.

To hang pots on walls or suspend them on chains from the walls, here's a sample of some of the brackets available today:

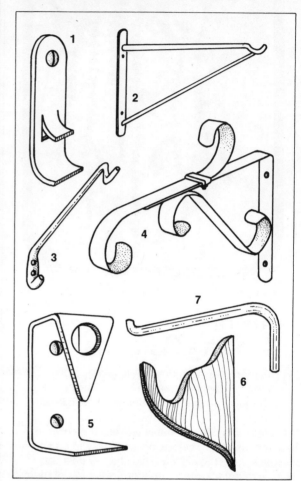

1 A small metal clip that fits on the rim of a clay pot.

2 Wrought-iron wall bracket.

3 Wall hook in brass.

4 Wrought-iron hook; the top hook slides back and forth.

5 Another version of a pot clip.

6 Wooden bracket used for hanging curtains on poles.

7 A lucite wall bracket.

In addition to the above, try utility-shelf brackets from the hardware store. Many of the items used in the installation of curtains and draperies offer more possibilities.

To fasten rope, twine or chain directly to a pot rim, make the following little clip from wire coat hangers, using three or four per pot.

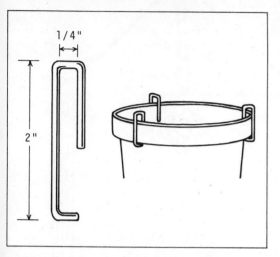

You can buy galvanized wire, snap-on hangers for clay pots that snap securely to four-inch to ten-inch pots. They are used extensively with orchids.

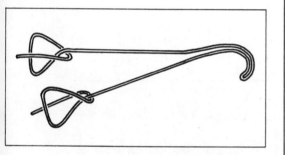

Or make some of your own out of aluminum clothes line:

Cut a piece about thirty inches long. Bend one end into a circle the size of the pot below the rim. Bend at a right angle and hook the circular piece. Bend the long piece to make the hanger and bring it back and hook on the opposite end of the circle.

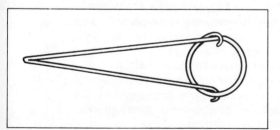

For this type of hanger, you should make a drip pan. Use a plastic saucer or a cake tin and the ever-ready coat-hanger wire. Hang this on the pot rim and the drip problem is solved.

There are many new types of plant hangers continually hitting the marketplace. Try them out or make your own, using imagination, wire, fish line, and perseverance. Here are a few more projects to send you on your way.

Using wire, jar lids (enameled white), chicken wire and a filling of sphagnum moss, you can make an inexpensive and unique hanging planter. Bend the top and bottom wires into hooks, and hang up a tier of them. They're great with hanging plants, and are just watered and fertilized by dunking.

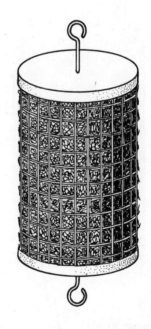

Or with heavy twine and those large wooden beads from a variety store, make a woven pot container:

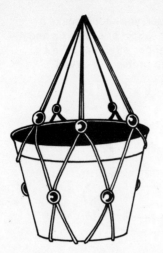

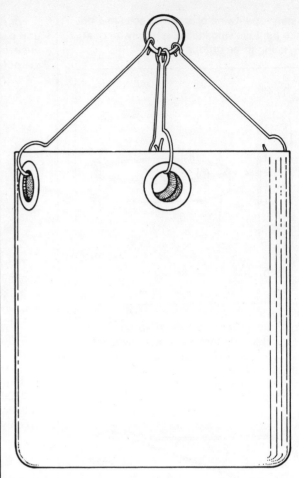

Or, using a six-inch clay pot and a six-inch eye-bolt, you may fashion the following hanging pot that will not leak on the floor. Slip a metal washer and a rubber washer on the bolt shaft, put it through the drainage hole, add another rubber washer, a metal washer and tighten with a nut. When potting add at least an inch of pebbles or shards to prevent water-logged soil.

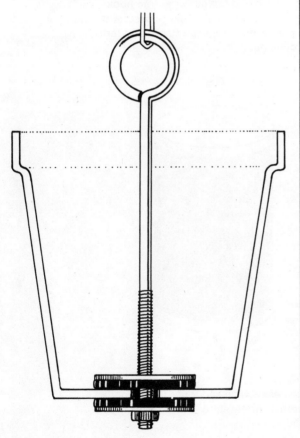

A very good friend of mine, now an active coordinator for political campaigns, once worked as an editorial advisor for a homemaker-type idea-and-fun magazine. One of the most revolting ideas she received from an avid reader was the manufacture of jewelry from dried chicken bones with pasted sequins. When I looked ill, she immediately came up with another: take an empty plastic bleach bottle and cut off the top; coat with glue or shellac, sprinkle with dust from a vacuum cleaner bag, and make a felt vase! True, it gives new meaning to the phrase, "waste not, want not" but bleach bottles have always been an anathema in my eyes.

So it is with some trepidation that I illustrate the following planter made from a cut-down bleach bottle and four brass grommets. It's simple in design and execution but is very effective with complex leaf patterns.

GROUND IVY

The first selection is a small member of the great "weed" family. Gill-over-the-ground or ground ivy (*Glecoma hederacea*) is a European immigrant that is found in waste areas throughout the northern United States and southern Canada. It's a bore to the purist lawn lover, but a beautiful ground cover to the rest. The name "gill" is from the French *guiller* and refers to its ancient use as hops in flavoring ale. From April to June, small blue-purple flowers emerge from the leaf axils.

Mine is potted in standard soil mix. It likes partial shade and the soil should be kept evenly moist. A big basket of gill is very attractive and inexpensive, since most gardeners are delighted to get rid of it. I took an old wine bottle and removed the top with one of the new glass-cutter kits, and inserted a three-inch clay pot.

A species with variegated leaves is offered by many plant houses, called *G. hederacea variegata*.

KENILWORTH IVY

Another European import that was originally used as a garden flower but has escaped to cover most of the area inhabited by ground ivy, is kenilworth ivy (*Cymbalaria muralis*).

This is a charming plant with tiny flowers that look like miniature snapdragons and it flowers throughout the year. It also seeds throughout the year and the small seed pods burst and shoot the seeds to every conceivable spot. It's often found growing in the mortar or in cracks between moist stones in old country walls. Most greenhouse owners consider it a pest and gladly give away great hunks of it. Use evenly moist standard mix and partial shade.

Mine grows within a plastic cover from a technical pen set, bolted to a mending strap and hung on the side of a window. It will soon need thinning, but I just attack it with a small sissors, and it immediately grows back.

FLORIST'S SMILAX

Florist's smilax (*Asparagus asparagoides myrtifolius*) is a fresh green vine with one-inch leaves. It's grown by florists to provide greens for bouquets and is a member of the asparagus family. Although technically a vine, I use it as a hanging plant and have set its pot in a Mexican gourd where the stems wind around the fish-line

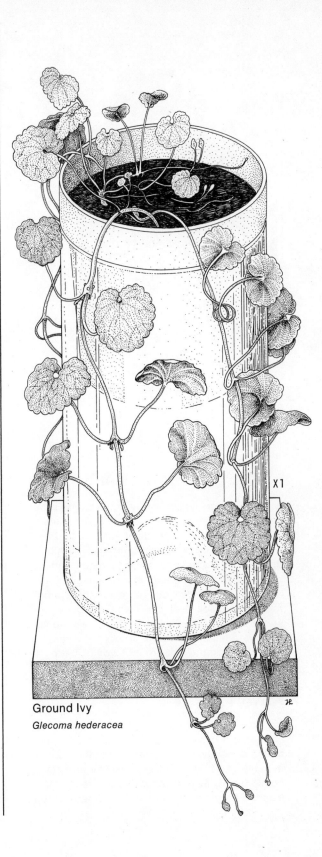

X 1

Ground Ivy
Glecoma hederacea

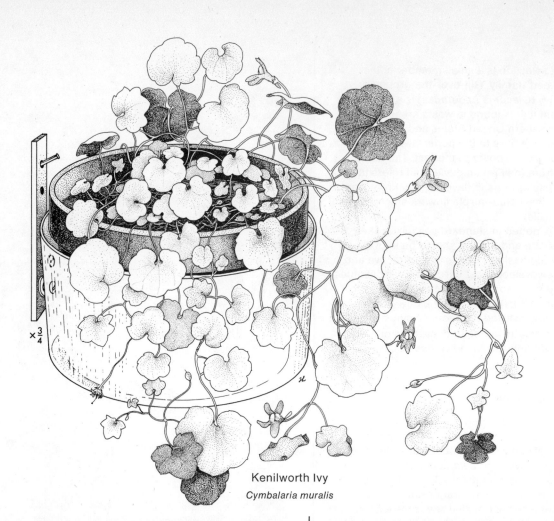

Kenilworth Ivy
Cymbalaria muralis

wires. It prefers its soil to dry out between waterings and the standard mix is fine. It, too, must be shielded from the midday heat of the sun.

Smilax prefers a warmer temperature than the first two plants, and doesn't like to go much below 60°F. Watch out for spider mites!

If you let it dry out, don't throw it out. Cut off the stems to soil level, give it water and see if it sprouts again. Usually, the roots are very tenacious and hold an amazing amount of water for their size, and the first drought won't kill the plant.

PRAYER PLANT

Red-veined prayer plant (*Maranta leuconeura erythroneura*) is a member of a tropical family that fold their leaves at night, hence their common name. Three species are widely grown as house plants (*M. leuconeura kerchoveana, M. leuconeura massangeana* are the other two) but

the red-veined is a most beautiful and rewarding sight. Its leaves grow up to five inches and exhibit a herringbone design of carmine-red veins over a velvety olive green to a lighter green at the leaf edge. The center is a silver-green. When happy, they produce tiny lilac flowers on eight-inch stems. They prefer a warm and moist atmosphere, with evenly moist soil (standard mix) and take a rest in the winter. New growth proceeds with the coming spring.

Maranta is usually grown as a table plant but, to me, it looks its best when the striking leaves seem to float in the air. Another reason could be the amount of time it took me to fashion a wall container out of half a coconut shell. I used an electric drill after clamping the shell with a vise to the working table edge. This, of course, after trying a brace-and-bit with nothing to hold the shell. The edge, in a continuing struggle, was evened with a hand saw. It's bolted to an angle iron. I think that this little exercise proves that al-

Florist's Smilax
Asparagus
asparagoides
myrtifolius

X1

most anything can be used for a container if perseverance is the key note.

If humidity is low, it's a good idea to spray the leaves with a mister every day.

QUEEN'S TEARS

Queen's tears (*Billbergia nutans*) is a member of the bromeliad group of pineapple fame. It's included here (and not with others of its kind) because it's such an old-fashioned house plant that demands next to nothing in care and really makes a statement when filling an eight-inch hanging pot.

An epiphyte, naturally growing on trees, this plant is no stranger to the air. The outer sides of the leaves are covered with a fine silvery powder which helps in absorbing water from the air. I try to mist the leaves, when I remember, and thoroughly water the plant every two weeks at least. It likes partial shade and temperatures from 50°F. up to 85°. I've wintered it at 45° and as long as the temperature change is not too abrupt, it doesn't mind a bit.

In late winter, the blooms appear: an arching stem wrapped in a cerise bract (a leaf that takes on coloring to act as a substitute or extra flower petal) shoots out of the leaf rosettes and bears a cluster of greenish flowers edged with a violet stripe. Each blossom bears a drop of nectar on the end of the stigma, hence the popular name.

Mine is potted in osmunda fiber alone. The pot in the picture is about to crack, and with the new shoots of this growing season will be divided and repotted. I use an orchid-type wire hanger and a plastic drip catcher hung with coat-hanger wire. The offshoots may be rooted in moist sphagnum moss. The plant is disease resistant (except for scale) due to the tough leaves.

MOONVINE

Moonvine (*Ipomoea noctiflora*) is an annual vine. This outstanding member of the morning-glory family produces large white fragrant flowers that open on cloudy afternoons or in early evening; they fold up and die by early morning.

Easily grown as a vine in any sunny window, I prefer them as hanging plants that can be moved about the house when blooming. Most people are enchanted with the flowers and a summer evening's entertainment becomes a

X3/4

Red-veined Prayer Plant
Maranta leuconeura erythroneura

X1

memorable event when the dining table is placed near a display of flowering moonvines.

Large seeds are quick to germinate if the seed coat is nicked with a nail file and soaked in water for twenty-four hours. Use Jiffy-7's as moonvines don't like direct disturbance of their roots. In winter, use a heating cable to speed germination; seeds should sprout within four days.

Plant in the standard potting mix, give as much sun as possible, and keep the watering can handy, as they wilt quickly on hot days.

If you are fast with a Q-Tip, experiment with cross-pollination. The developing seed pods are unique and interesting to watch.

Moonvine or moonflower is a perennial but it is easier to grow new plants from seed than hold them over the winter in pots. It's also known by the name *Calonyction aculeatum*.

LANTANA

A basket plant grown for years is lantana (*Lantana camara*). It's really a shrub and has escaped from cultivation in many areas of the Deep South. While driving in central Florida, I saw miles of lantana in full bloom, growing between roadside ditches and orange groves.

The flowers are yellow when they open, turn orange and then red. All three colors are evident in the same cluster. If flowers are not clipped off, small black berries may develop. The leaves are supposed to give off an objectionable odor when crushed, but it should not bother anyone,

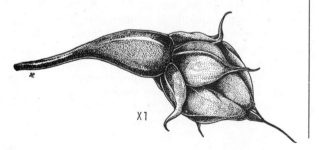

X1

X1/2

X1

Queen's Tears
Billbergia nutans

unless crushing leaves is your thing. Pinch back the stem tips for bushy growth. Lantana flowers throughout the summer and occasionally in wintertime, if given enough light. This plant enjoys full sun, warm temperature (70°F.) and the soil should be allowed to dry, but not completely, between waterings.

To grow a lantana tree buy a small plant, preferably one with only one shoot. Plant in a three-inch pot and tie to a foot-long bamboo cane or

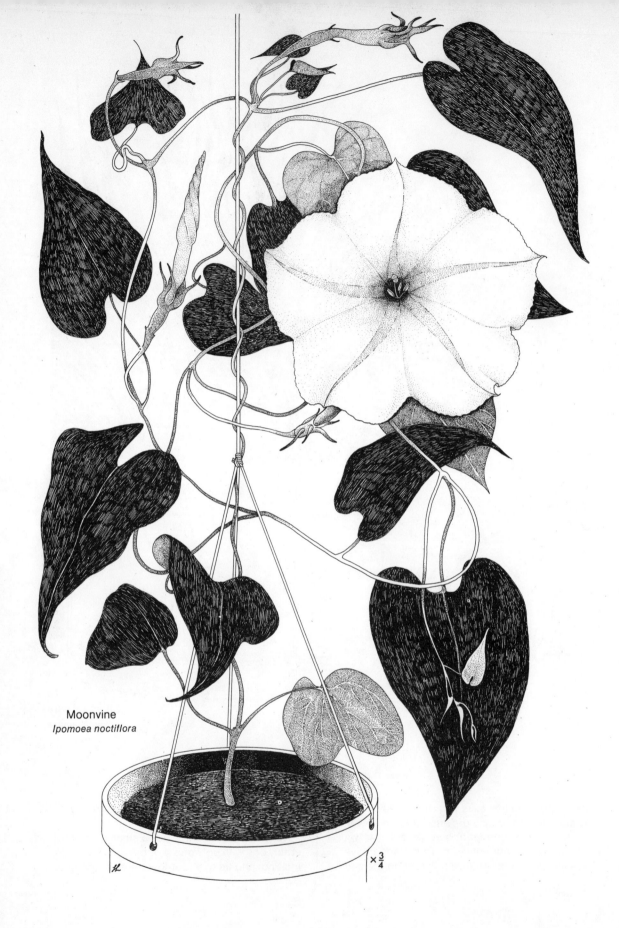

Moonvine
Ipomoea noctiflora

one section of a Reef Flower Stake Holder. Use one circle of soft cord about the stem and one loop about the stake; never tie any plant directly to a support. If growing from seed, be prepared for a wait, as germination may take two months or more.

When the plant reaches about ten inches, move to a five- or six-inch pot. Add a second length to the Reef apparatus or use a thirty-inch bamboo stake. Now remove all the side shoots, leaving just the terminal bud.

As the lantana approaches two feet, move it to an eight-inch pot. All the time you've been forcing it to grow upward, the root system has been growing, too. Pinch off the terminal bud. As new side shoots appear, pinch off their terminal buds, forcing bushy growth. The stem will develop a woody look and you'll have a beautiful flowering tree. The process may take two years, but it's worth it.

As the tree grows, it can be moved into bigger pots, or pruned every year. Top-dress the soil and fertilize during summer months.

In the north, lantanas must winter inside and will enter a dormant period.

The plant holder in the picture was made with a piece of sheet acrylic, cut with a saber saw. The pot rim should fit snugly into the opening. Plywood works well, too.

Propagate from seed or stem cuttings.

LOBELIA

Lobelia (*Lobelia erinus* 'Crystal Palace') has flowers of an intense blue and is used for edging in gardens during the summer. The leaves are a light green that develop a bronze cast in sunlight.

Dig up young plants in August and pot in the standard mix. In September, before a frost, bring them inside to a sunny window. Temperature should be about 70°F. during the day, cooler at night. With luck, they will flower until December.

Or you can start seeds in August for flowers by midwinter. The seeds take about twenty days to germinate and must have light to do so.

The pot pictured is held by a commercially available clip. The drain hole is sealed with a piece of plastic weatherstripping. The lobelia pot rests inside on a stone to prevent the soil from being too wet. Soil should be evenly moist.

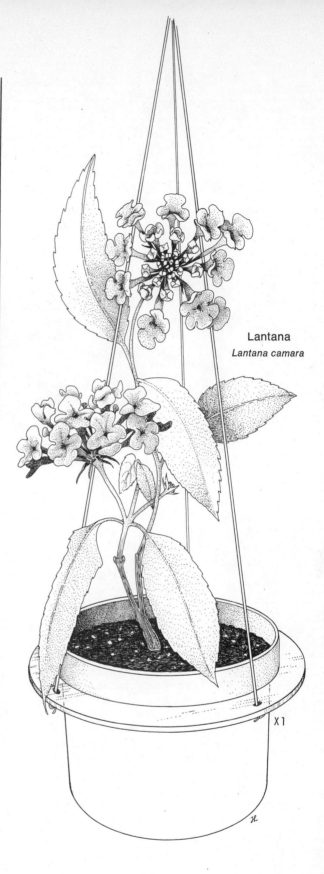

Lantana
Lantana camara

X 1

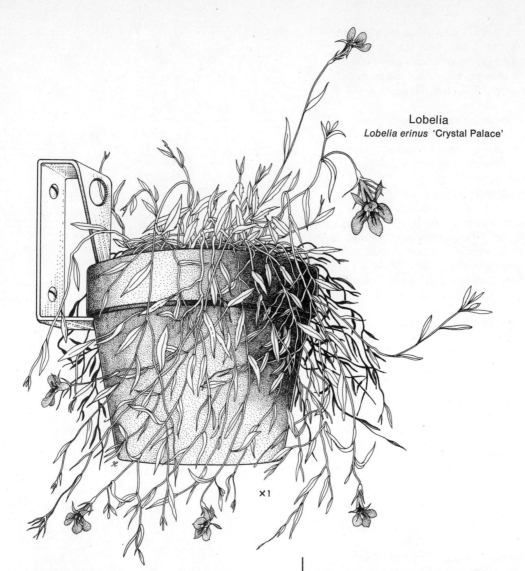

Lobelia
Lobelia erinus 'Crystal Palace'

×1

SPIDER PLANTS

Spider plants (*Chlorophytum comosum* 'Vitta-tum') are among the oldest of house plants and, for many people, familiarity causes extreme boredom. They miss a good bet, for a mature specimen of *Chlorophytum*, trailing dozens of smaller plants, is a spectacular sight.

The common name refers to the long, cascading runners, often over two feet long, that the mother plant produces with great regularity. Tiny bumps on the runners produce either tiny greenish-white flowers or baby plants. The plantlets will root in a moist medium or hang on the runners for years, increasing in size.

The roots are thick and fleshy, and in smaller pots, will push the plant right out of the soil. Keep the soil moist, but don't worry if you forget occasionally, since the roots can store quite a bit of water. It generally takes effort to injure these plants. Filtered light is preferred. Mist the leaves during the summertime and repot any time of the year. The standard soil mix is fine and feed them three or four times a year.

Chlorophytum comosum 'Vittatum' has pale green leaves with a white center stripe. *C. comosum* 'Variegatum' is a larger plant. Leaves average a foot in length and are edged in white.

SWEET POTATO

Sweet potatoes conjure up memories of childhood and rooting tubers in Mason jars of water. Today, they are rarer because of the common practice of kiln drying to give the vegetables added shelf life. When purchased in a supermarket, check for a live sprout. The best place to find these are at Farmer's Markets in the spring. You can root them in water—the only requirement is warmth and sun. Or plant the tubers in the standard mix, large end up (if there is a large end), or horizontally. Plant food should be added if grown in water, on a monthly basis. Remember too, not to let the tuber dry out. A healthy plant uses a great deal of water in the summer.

The Latin name is *Ipomoea batatas* (the sweet potato belongs to the morning-glory family). The flowers are two-inches long and funnel-shaped.

The container shown is a ceramic sweet-potato suspended with small black chains.

When started in water, cover only half the tuber. Propagate with rooted cuttings.

I. batatas 'Blackie' is an ornamental variety grown for its striking leaf color. The new leaves are green, but quickly turn to a rich, deep purple that is close to black, with wine-red undersides.

Man-of-the-Earth (*I. pandurata*) is a native member of this group. Aboveground, the vines produce white flowers up to three inches long, often with purple centers. Belowground is a truly massive root, weighing an average of twenty pounds and well over two feet long. If treated as a pot plant (in a very large pot), the vine dies each fall and the tuber must winter in cool (40°F.) temperatures. The North American Indians called it "Mecha-Meck" and roasted the tubers for food.

Man-of-the-Earth is found from Connecticut to southern Ontario, Michigan, Kansas, and south to Florida.

In addition, there are wild morning glories called bindweed that may be grown from collected seed, but take care: They are a very troublesome weed and gardeners will not thank you if you allow the plants to spread.

HELIOTROPE

Heliotrope (*Heliotropium speciosus*) has lovely racemes of flowers, which have a very strong and sweet fragrance reminiscent of vanilla. They are often used in summer gardens in the north and may be potted in August to bring inside before frost. Older specimens become shrubby, but young plants are great for hanging containers. They are propagated by cuttings or seed at any time of the year. Seeds planted the beginning of January bear flowers by early May. Use the standard potting mix, keep evenly moist and protect from the hot sun of summer. When growing, fertilize once a month.

Following the instructions for lantana, you can make a standard of heliotrope.

BASKET GRASS

Basket grass (*Oplismenus hirtellus variegatus*) is a creeping perennial grass from the tropics. The leaves are thin, lance-shaped, and striped with white and pink. The plants like 70°F. and should be kept evenly moist in the standard mix. Fertilize twice a month during the summer to prevent the leaves from scorching at the tips. They need full sun to provide the best color. Propagate new plants from rooted cuttings or just bending back a stem and sticking it in the pot.

WANDERING JEW

Zebrinas and *Tradescantias* are two distinct genera, each called wandering Jew, spiderworts or inch plants. They are all ever-popular hanging-basket plants requiring little attention. All, except for a few of the hybrids, like full sun. Temperatures should be around 70°F. and soil should be allowed to dry slightly between waterings. The illustration shows five different plants, all growing happily in one six-inch pot. They root easily with cuttings in moist sphagnum moss or water.

1 Bronze wandering Jew (*Zebrina purpusii*) has dark purple leaves that appear almost black with good light. Flowers are lavender. This plant is used extensively for public and private garden beds in the southern United States.

2 Tricolor wandering Jew (*Z. pendula* 'Discolor') has metallic purple and green leaves with silver striping. Flowers are purple.

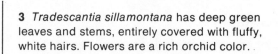

2

4

1

X3/4

3

5

3 *Tradescantia sillamontana* has deep green leaves and stems, entirely covered with fluffy, white hairs. Flowers are a rich orchid color.

4 *T. blossfeldiana* is a hairy plant with olive-green leaves. It blooms almost continually with white and purple flowers.

5 Wandering Jew (*T. fluminensis*) has bluish-green leaves, purple underneath, and white flowers.

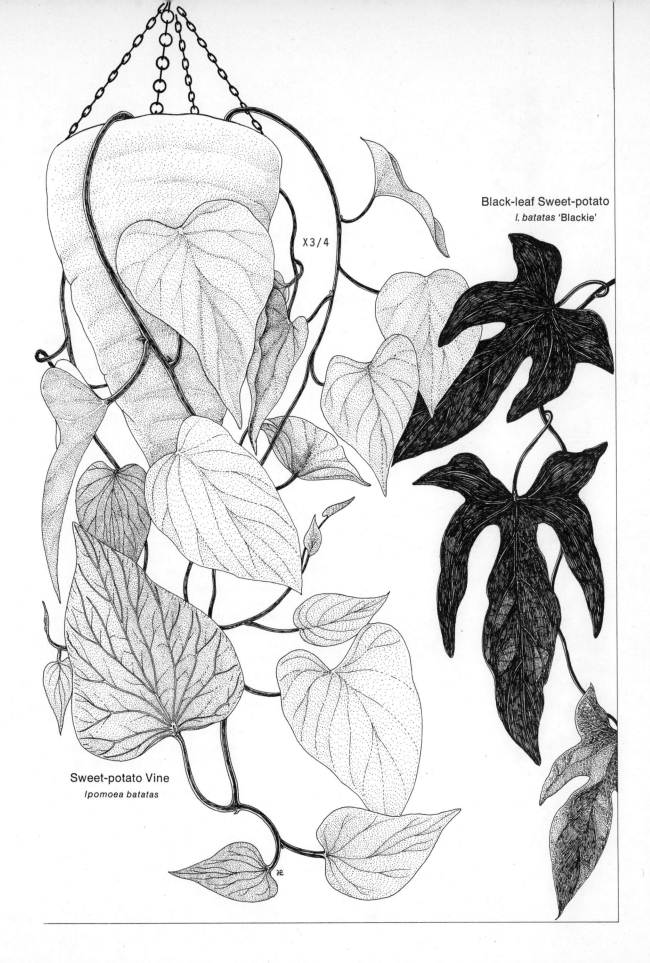

X3/4

Black-leaf Sweet-potato
I. batatas 'Blackie'

Sweet-potato Vine
Ipomoea batatas

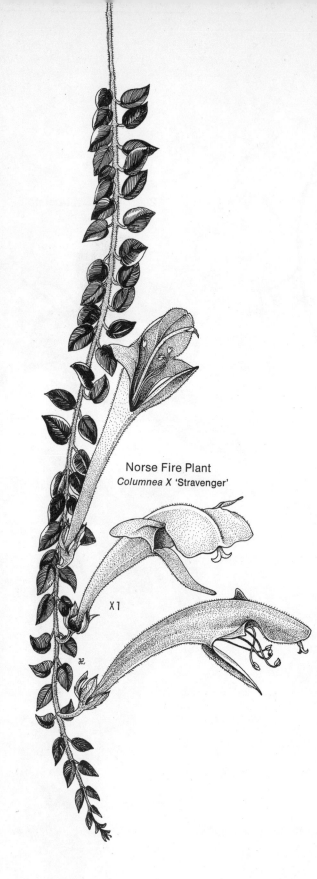

Norse Fire Plant
Columnea X 'Stravenger'

X1

COLUMNEA

Norse fire plant (*Columnea* x 'Stravenger') is a show-stopper. Four years ago, I started with a four-inch plant with five stems. This spring (the third year of blooms) there are thirty-five strands from four to six feet in length, each strand bearing an average of thirty brilliant orange flowers that look like Ollie the Dragon.

Since columnea are primarily epiphytic, mine is potted in a six-inch pot of pure osmunda fiber. I water every other day in summer, slow down in autumn and to about once a week in winter. Fertilizer is given every three weeks in summer only. Temperatures that have fallen to 45°F. at the roof of my sun porch in winter have never fazed this magnificent plant. It propagates easily with stem cuttings.

There are now so many hybrids of columnea that an indoor gardener can fill rooms and never look at another type of plant. I wish I had the room to expand my collection.

BEGONIA

For years I've admired hanging baskets of tree-fern fiber but the accepted way of watering was immersion (with minutes of dripping.) Not an acceptable container for a living room display. Then I found out about the water wick. By burying a small glass container in the earth within the fern pot, there have been no drips; the plant absorbs what it needs. I just refill the glass every day. The plant is a *Begonia rex* 'Comtesse Louise Erdoedy'. The common name is the corkscrew begonia. This is a rhizomatous begonia with a rhizome that creeps along the soil surface. A container with a wide top and a narrow bottom is excellent for this kind of plant growth.

Begonias have been studied and hybridized for years. The corkscrew begonia resulted from a cross between two *B. rex* hybrids in 1833 by the gardener to the Comte Erdoedy. Leaves grow to a foot in length, are light green, overcast with a silvery-rose sheen.

I use the standard soil mix, put the plant in partial shade and fertilize once a month. Begonias prefer warmth but winters in the sun porch are perfectly acceptable to the corkscrew as long as it's near the hot-air duct.

Corkscrew Begonia
Begonia rex 'Comtesse Louise Erdoedy'

X1/3

CHAPTER NINE
Cacti and Succulents

Many people think of cacti as giant, spiny heaps that sombrero-clad Mexicans lean upon, or little pin balls that fill ceramic pots painted to represent burro carts. It's an unfortunate outlook. Some of the world's most beautiful flowers appear on what can be termed truly bizarre-and-unique plant growths, and if simple cultural demands are met, satisfaction is guaranteed.

I've kept cactus and succulents for about four years. The first was a peanut cactus (*Chamaecereus silvestri*) that my wife rescued from a radiator top during her first year of teaching. It was in a small plastic pot wedged between two blackboard erasers and a set of warped wooden blocks. It was so brown and misshapen, I couldn't tell what kind of cactus it was. Water, a scrub brush and repotting soon restored it to a semblance of its former self, and it now fills a six-inch pot and flowers every April.

Naturally, I was bitten by the cactus bug and slowly increased my collection to include both cactus and succulents, most of which are described in this chapter.

What's the difference between cacti and succulents? Both are *xerophytes*, or plants that

have adapted to survival under conditions of a limited water supply.* Both groups are termed succulent, because they have developed thick, fleshy, water-storing stems or leaves. However, all cacti belong to one family and are the only plants that produce an *areole*. This is a spot on the plant consisting of a tuft of wool or hair that produces spines and, in most cases, flowers. In addition, cacti have given up leaves to gain the spines, with one exception: the genus *Pereskia*, a large plant from Mexico with flowers like a rose, and very large leaves. Finally, most cacti originated in the New World.

Succulent is not a family name but applies to many plants from all over the world. If a plant has the ability to store water in its leaves or stems, it's a succulent regardless of what family it belongs to.

GENERAL CARE

Unless the individual plants described have unique demands, the following rules apply to all.

Watering

Cacti and succulents *do* approve of water. When in small pots under the summer sun, you might have to water every day. And this leads to the next requirement: Never give water until the soil is dry—overwatering will quickly rot the roots. Water from the top only and empty all saucers of excess. Since many of these plants come from warm climates, they are sent into a dormant period by lack of rain, so at the beginning of winter, keep the plants in a cool place between 40° and 50°F. Start watering again in early spring, as the days start to get longer.

Light

Most of these plants will eke out a wretched existence without sunlight and take a very long time to expire completely. However, to produce flowers they must have at least three hours of direct sun a day. But since many of these plants are shaded by others when growing in the deserts of the world, direct sun all day is not necessary.

---

*A few cacti are now found growing in jungles where water is hardly a problem (e.g. the orchid cactus), but eons ago, those areas were desert; the plants have slowly evolved to accept ample water and still keep their succulent characteristics.

Soil and Potting

The recipe:
1/4 loam or packaged soil
1/4 leaf mold or peat moss
1/4 sand
1/4 gravel or small pieces of broken pots.

Depending on how much soil you are mixing, add up to a pint of bone meal for a bushel of soil. Since drainage is an absolute necessity for these plants, pot them with plenty of crocking as seen in the illustration.

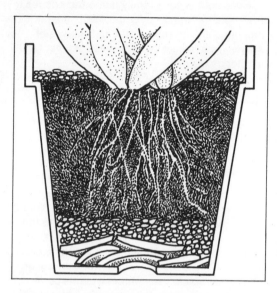

The best time to pot cacti is in early spring or when new growth starts. Succulents can be potted at any time they are in active growth. Some plants might require potting once a year. To prevent sore fingers, hold the cactus in a folded piece of paper when transplanting the spiny varieties.

Once the plant is out of the pot, remove some of the old soil. Dead and broken roots should be cut off with a sharp, clean knife. Never go up more than one pot size, and make sure the plant is placed so the new soil comes exactly to the original level. Soil should be firm, not packed with violence, and come to about three-quarters of an inch from the pot rim. A top dressing of gravel will help to keep the soil from major disturbance from watering. Don't water for about a week. I realize all this sounds very fussy, but most of these plants have tiny, hair-like roots that are easily damaged and should not be given water until they can heal.

Addition of Fertilizer

There are many schools of thought on the addition of fertilizers to cacti and succulents. I never give any to mine, since they are repotted at least every two years. They grow well and flower, so I don't think it's necessary. The one exception is the Christmas cactus (*Schlumbergera bridgesii*) which has been in the same pot for almost four years, and every summer I give it a few shots of plant food as a reward for its yearly blooms.

Taking Plants Outside

Most of the cacti and succulents will benefit from a season in the outdoor air, and their pots may be placed directly in the garden area, if there is sufficient drainage under each pot to allow for heavy rains. A slight frost should not hurt the ground dwellers as the desert is very cold at night. Freezing is a different story. During the desert winters, these plants have very little water and are usually blanketed with a mantle of insulating snow.

As domesticated plants, however, they will probably receive an unnatural amount of water and if exposed to more than an hour or so of freezing cold they will be killed by the expansive action of the ice.

Check for slugs and red spider mites before bringing the plants back indoors.

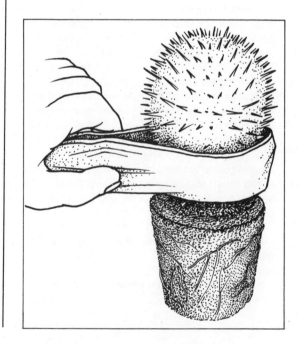

ORCHID CACTUS

Because most people know what the typical cactus looks like, a ball with spines, and the average succulent is thought to be a jade plant from the five and ten, I decided to show the more unusual plants in these families. It's generally considered bad form to begin with the most spectacular, but I find all these plants either so beautiful or so intriguing that I'll start with the most magnificent of them all—the orchid cacti (*Epiphyllum* x *hybridus*).

Epiphyllums are the "ugly duckling" most of the year since they consist of long, flat, straplike stems of a pleasant but not outstanding green, a few tiny spines, and nothing else. They do have an architectural look about them when large, but this is not reason enough to keep them around. But with the coming of spring, tiny buds appear along stems that are one or two years old. Each day the buds grow larger until finally, the most breathtaking blossoms appear. There are hundreds of hybrids available and colors range from pure white to yellow, pink, satiny red, and deep purples. Sizes range from a demure three-inch diameter to a stunning ten-inch blossom.

Mine is an unnamed hybrid of deep and iridescent carmine and measures six inches across.

Epiphyllums are very easy to care for. I started with a four-inch cutting in 1971. By late '72 there were four two-foot straps and I eagerly looked forward to the spring of '73 for blooms, as I didn't know what color or size they would be. Unfortunately, early in '73 we had a freak windstorm that broke a window and literally pulverized the stems. They were so bruised and beaten, that I cut them off and resigned myself to another wait. In 1974, it bloomed carmine red and the wait was forgotten.

In nature, these plants hang from trees or rest on the ground and are considered to be epiphytes. My wife made a small clay pot with one drain hole that hangs by an east window. In summer, I move it outdoors under a large black cherry, so it's shaded during the hottest part of the day. Because the orchid cactus grows in tree crotches in the wild, I potted it in undiluted osmunda fiber and I do not fertilize it. The osmunda was changed this year right after blooming stopped. The stems are misted occasionally during the warm days of spring and fall. I water when the stems show any sign of shriveling. From November to February, the plant is moved to the sun porch, where temperatures have fallen as low as 40°F., and it hasn't been harmed.

Orchid cacti may also be potted in the cactus mix, but if you cannot hang them out-of-doors in the summer or if you have a dry year, you'll have to water and mist them more often.

To propagate, take four-inch cuttings, let them air-dry for a few days, then root in moist sphagnum or peat moss during spring and summer.

DRUNKARD'S DREAM

Another epiphytic cactus, of easy culture and smaller habit than the orchid cactus, is drunkard's dream (*Hatiora salicornioides*). The jointed stems are a fresh grassy green, strongly resembling small bottles, with smaller bottles growing from the caps. Under strong light, tiny purple spots appear along the stems with no regular pattern. Spines are reduced to minute patches of fuzz in the bottle-cap position. Two years ago, my plant was about five inches across; now it's a fountain of green, over sixteen inches in width.

In early spring, butterscotch-yellow flowers appear at the tip of each stem. They have a waxy shine and never completely open. It's a welcome sight with snow on the ground.

Fruit will occasionally develop; it's a translucent white with a shiny red nose, hence the name.

Hatiora requires a truly moist atmosphere at all times and a fairly rich compost, so I use the standard succulent soil mix instead of osmunda, and change every two years. Mist the plant at least once a day and keep the soil evenly moist. This is a good candidate for a self-watering wick or one of the Riviera pots. It takes full sun all winter but should have partial shade during the hot summer months.

DISH GARDENS

Growers who collect and display large numbers of cacti and succulents are usually loath to put them in dish gardens of any type, but to keep a small collection it's the obvious answer. Dishes should be glazed (to protect furniture from water stains) and as plain in decorative effects as possible. Striking patterns, busy patterns and bombastic colors detract from the fragile colors of many of these plants. Drainage holes are not really necessary, if an adequate layer of crockery and stones underlies the soil. When possible, pick a container that is deep enough to hold individual pots without removing the plants. This allows greater freedom in

X1

Orchid Cactus
Epiphyllum x hybridus

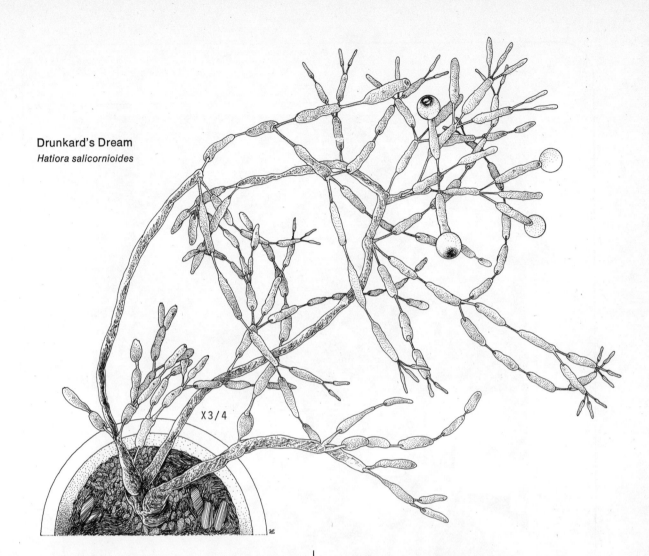

Drunkard's Dream
Hatiora salicornioides

X 3/4

arrangements, and if one plant grows too quickly, it's easily removed and another substituted.

Most succulents when in full growth take a sizable amount of water, but care must be taken not to overdo. Wet soil will quickly rot the roots. When in doubt, don't water at all. Some varieties may shrivel a bit, but make a quick recovery on the next watering.

Plants in an arrangement should all have the same cultural requirements. The following garden works very well—the only problem is the good-luck plant, which has a tendency to spread rapidly.

1 Plover's eggs (*Acromischus festivus*) looks just like its name. The succulent leaves are mottled with maroon spots and small red flowers appear in late spring. As with most succulents, when one of the leaves is jarred loose, it will generally root with ease.

2 *Cotyledon orbiculata oophylla* has no common name. The leaves are a gray-green and are covered with a dusting of fine white powder. Individual leaves will root quickly.

3 Copper rose (*Echeveria multicaulis*) is a many-branched plant which grows to about eight inches. It has waxy leaves of a coppery brown edged with a deeper brown.

4 Panda plant (*Kalanchoe tomentosa*) has three-inch leaves entirely covered with a soft, white felt, the edges burned with brown. As the plant ages, aerial roots appear from the stem to help support the plant.

5 Good-luck plant (*K. daigremontiana* x *tubiflora*) has pinkish-brown leaves that support tiny new plants all along the edges. As they drop they root, and in a short time everyone you know will be able to refuse a dozen or two.

X1

6 Jelly beans (*Sedum pachyphyllum*) looks enough like its namesake to take a place in an Easter basket. Each "bean" is about an inch and a half long, and the branches bend easily under the weight; they root when striking the ground.

AURORA BOREALIS PLANT

When aurora (*Kalanchoe fedtschenkoi marginata*) is grown in full sun, the margins of the blue-green leaves turn a lovely shade of pink; when kept in partial shade they remain white. Coral pink flowers with four petals form in late winter and remain on the plant until spring. The buds have a silky sheen and you never think they'll open. They need a few hours of winter sunlight in order to bloom. In time, the stem becomes very calloused and looks like a miniature tree trunk. Aerial roots form to hold up the growing stem.

This plant does not like a great deal of water. If the leaves become limp, water. If they yellow and drop, you're giving too much.

The small plants at the pot bottom are leaves that have dropped and rooted, so you'll have no problems adding more of these plants to your collection.

GREEN MARBLE VINE

The marble vine (*Senecio herreianus*) is a great plant for small apartments. The leaves grow to three-quarters of an inch as they mature and form a seemingly endless chain of beads as they creep along the soil and over the edge of the pot.

If you examine a leaf closely, you'll see a thin translucent area that acts as a window to insure the maximum amount of light for each bead.

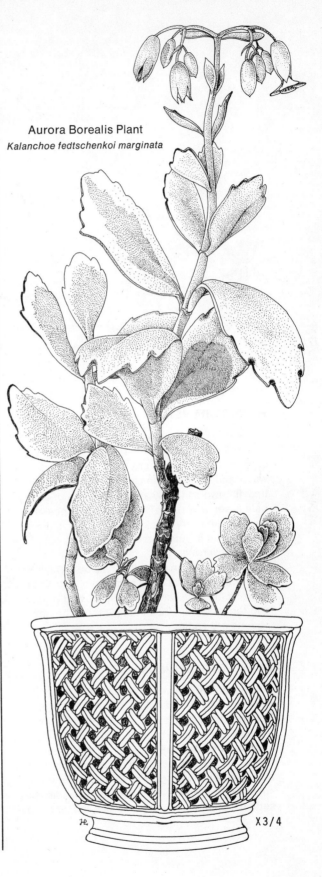

Aurora Borealis Plant
Kalanchoe fedtschenkoi marginata

X 3 / 4

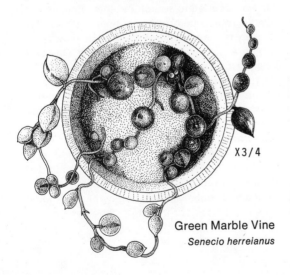

X 3 / 4

Green Marble Vine
Senecio herreianus

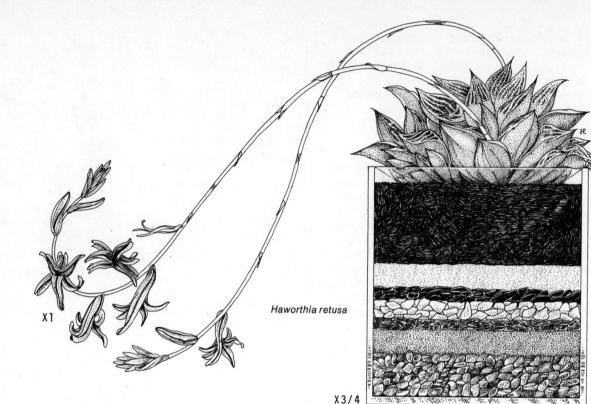

X1

Haworthia retusa

X 3 / 4

HAWORTHIA RETUSA

There is no common name for this little succulent, but it is so charming it doesn't really deserve one. The leaves are thick with stored water and marked with clear windows at their tips. It flowers in early spring in colors of a very pale green and pink. This plant announces thirst by shriveling very quickly, and does not like hot midday sun in summer. Broken leaves will sprout new roots.

Mine is potted in a small acrylic box which has different layers of stones and gravel. I used bird gravel, charcoal, sand, white sand, and perlite, and topped it with the standard mix. The combinations are endless.

BLACK TREE AEONIUM

This succulent (*Aeonium arboreum atropurpureum*) will reach a height of three feet in time. The rosette of leaves remains a light green but becomes purple as the light increases. This is another succulent that dislikes very hot sun at noon during summer, so give it some shade. It also likes a little more water than most in the summer and signals its needs by the whole rosette drooping. If you get tired of a tall plant, just cut it at the height desired and reroot in a moist medium of spagnum or peat. The leaves will also root, if they are fresh. The stem develops a beautiful brownish texture with age.

HOTTENTOT FIG

Two springs ago, my wife and I visited Florida, and stopped at Daytona Beach (two years ago it was still a beach). While walking along the edge of the dunes, I noticed a very unusual succulent, growing in and under the sand. I took home a broken piece and potted it in the succulent mix and proceeded to search out the name. My cactus reference books mentioned a plant that closely resembled it but the area given was South Africa, so I was a bit confused. One day I looked it up in the *Exotic Plant Manual* (see Bibliography) and found the explanation. Apparently the state of Florida or the U.S. Government was using the plant as a sand-binder. It's supposed to bloom with a large, yellow flower like a daisy and produce edible fruit. The Latin name is *Carpobrotus edulis* and it's the most undemanding plant I have ever had. If you find a broken piece on a sub-tropical beach, take it home and roots will form in any medium. Mine has yet to flower or fruit, but I'll be patient.

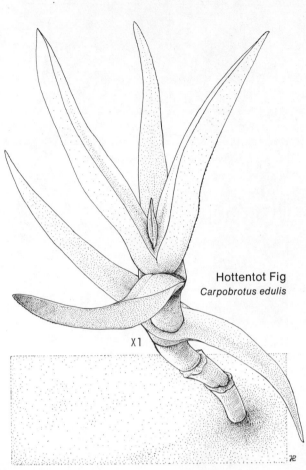

Hottentot Fig
Carpobrotus edulis

X 1

Black Tree Aeonium
*Aeonium arboreum
atropurpureum*

X 3 / 4

SEMPERVIVUM POT GARDEN

Sempervivums are common rock-garden plants throughout the United States. Hens and Chickens is the catch-all name for most of those grown. The breeding and collecting of these plants can become a full-time hobby in itself, and many nurseries now stock a number of named varieties. They like to be watered in the summer months, but you can depend on the rain if pots are left outside. My pot is watered once in the winter, about the time of the January thaw, and I don't think it's necessary then. The only requirement is a period of relative cold in the winter. These plants will not do very well if

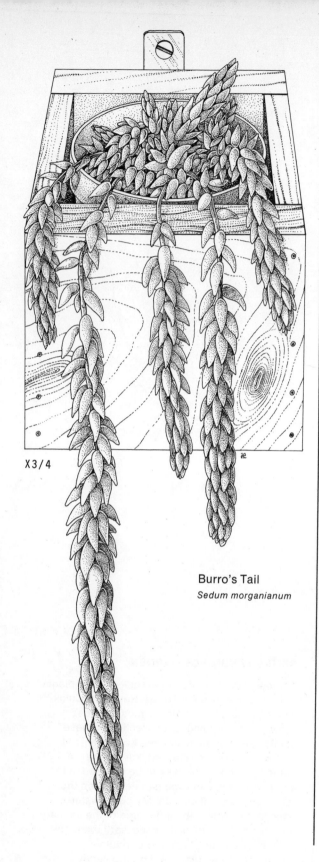

X 3/4

Burro's Tail
Sedum morganianum

denied a temperature drop. You can easily solve the problem by placing plants next to a cold window.

1 *Sempervivum atropurpureum* is about four inches in diameter and a most beautiful purplish color when given full sun.

2 *S. braunii* are one-inch rosettes of bright green with brown tips.

3 *S. arachnoideum* comes from Europe and is called the cobweb houseleek. The rosettes are tightly packed with leaves and average an inch in diameter. In winter, the rosettes are bare, but with spring, you an watch tiny webs form over their tops. These webs act as summer protection from the sun.

4 *Echeveria pulvinata* is an interloper that I planted to take the place of another sedum that went to a friend. It can only stay in the pot if I make sure frost is not allowed. The leaves are pale green, edged with red and covered with white hairs.

5 *S. atroviolaceum* forms a very large rosette with shades of violet.

Since this pot was prepared last fall, I expect an additional bonus of flowers on all the sempervivums this year. The echeveria flowers every spring, and often in the summer, too, with a tall spray of bright orange flowers that work very well in dried flower arrangements.

CARRION FLOWER

Stapelia variegata or the carrion flower (or the spotted toad cactus, depending on your point of view) is one member of a truly bizarre family of succulents. Don't let the name turn you off. They have a rather obnoxious odor if you push your nose directly into the flower's face, but you won't notice anything from a distance. These are a family of African milkweeds, and if pollenated by a passing fly (bees will turn the other way) the bursting seed pods look exactly like the American milkweed.

The flowers are up to three inches across and every part is in units of five. The color is greenish-yellow with maroon spots and attracts attention (for visual reasons) whenever it blooms.

X 3/4

Stapelia root easily from cuttings. They need winter sun to flower and cooler temperatures.

Last year I grew a *Stapelia hirsuta* or the hairy star fish flower but my family asked me to give it up, as they did notice the smell.

BURRO'S TAIL

It was a toss-up whether to include burro's tail (*Sedum morganianum*) in the chapter on hanging plants or here. Since it is both, but known

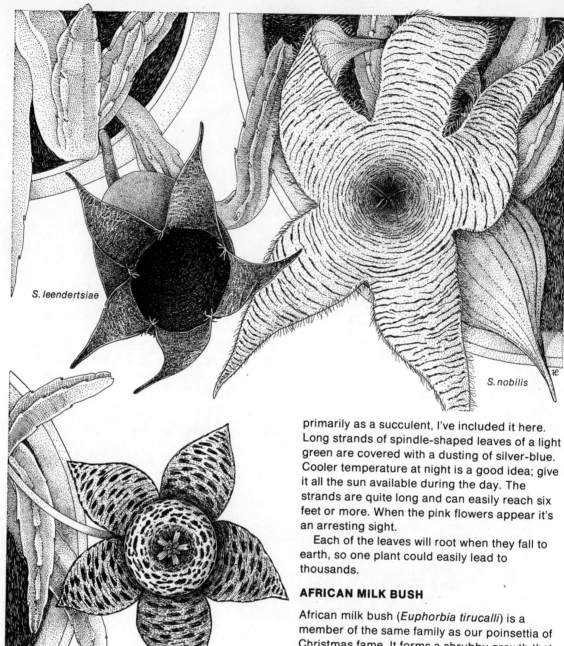

S. leendertsiae

S. nobilis

Stapelia variegata

X 3/4

primarily as a succulent, I've included it here. Long strands of spindle-shaped leaves of a light green are covered with a dusting of silver-blue. Cooler temperature at night is a good idea; give it all the sun available during the day. The strands are quite long and can easily reach six feet or more. When the pink flowers appear it's an arresting sight.

Each of the leaves will root when they fall to earth, so one plant could easily lead to thousands.

AFRICAN MILK BUSH

African milk bush (*Euphorbia tirucalli*) is a member of the same family as our poinsettia of Christmas fame. It forms a shrubby growth that reaches twenty feet or more in the wilds of the Congo. Mine is now four-and-one-half feet high and going strong. You've got to be careful with this one if curious children are around as the milky sap is poisonous. Each spring it grows a new crop of tiny leaves that fall by the end of summer. It's a beautiful decorator plant. Since they become top-heavy, staking is usually necessary. I've used a Reef Flower Pot Stake Holder for support, as it is an unobtrusive and inventive method of holding tall and weak stems.

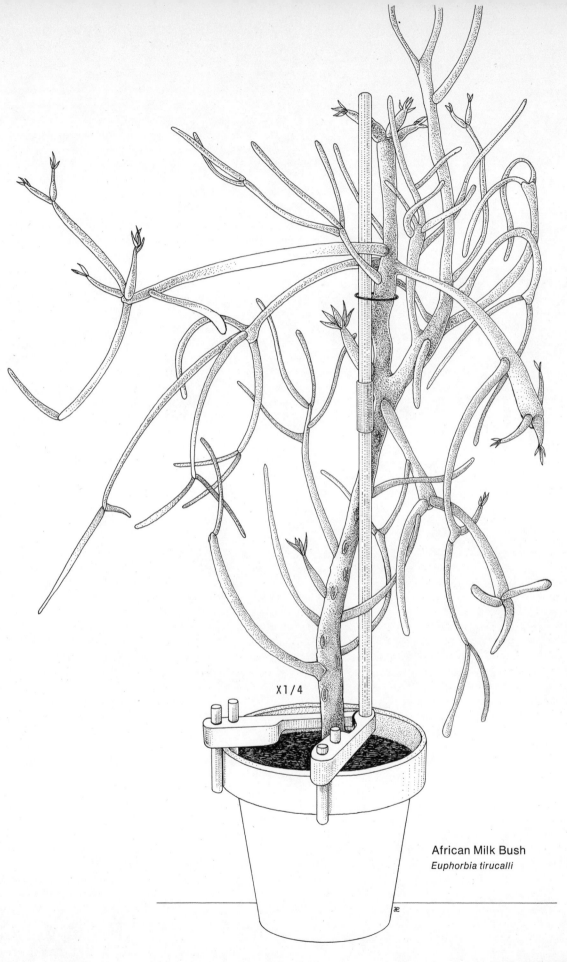

X1/4

African Milk Bush
Euphorbia tirucalli

CHAPTER TEN
Exotics

Exotic simply means "of foreign origin or character; something or someone introduced from overseas." The majority of house plants grown today will meet this definition. Exotic also means "striking or unusual in effect or appearance; strange, exciting, and glamorous," and among the plants that answer to this description, count in orchids and bromeliads. And, despite their reputation, these two genera of plants have representative types that are among the easiest of plants to grow.

BROMELIADS

There are two basic types of bromeliads; epiphytes, plants that live aloft in trees, on vines, or on other epiphytes; and the terrestrial plants with well-developed root systems. All share one characteristic that differentiates them from other plants: the presence of scales on the leaf surface to absorb water and minerals from rain, dew, fog, or mist. The pineapple plant (*Anana comosus*) lives on the ground, and the scales are very insignificant, although easily visible under a hand lens. Water and nourishment is taken up through a well-developed root system.

Tillandsias are epiphytes and are covered with obvious scales, their poorly developed root systems functioning as holdfasts. Because of these scales, most epiphytic bromeliads are extremely adaptable to variations in water, and easily survive in overheated rooms if they are misted daily. In addition, the leaves of many bromeliads form little reservoirs, storing water for future use.

The terrestrial varieties are a bit more choosy and like the conditions usually found on the jungle floor—moist but not soggy soil and reasonable humidity. Most terrestrials do well in potted osmunda fiber or peat moss. A monthly shot of liquid fertilizer to the growing medium is generally beneficial as the jungle floor is rich in decayed organic matter.

EPIPHYTIC BROMELIADS

The first illustration shows a piece of weathered log, found after a lumbering operation in a northern woods. Rain, wind, and sun have turned the surface to a cracked and pitted silver-gray. By drilling three-quarter and one-inch-diameter holes about two inches deep, and packing them with osmunda, I have a beautiful and naturalistic setting for seven tillandsias. In summer, the planter is set outside beneath a small tree, shading the plants from the noonday sun. Each morning dew covers the leaves allowing the minute scales that cover the undersurface all the water needed for healthy growth.

Before the first frost, the planter comes indoors to the sun porch, where it's put in the brightest spot. Temperatures fluctuate all winter, going down to 45°F. Since Florida is the home of most of these bromeliads, they are not bothered a bit. The leaves are misted every few days. Never fertilize epiphytic bromeliads—just repack the osmunda every two to three years.

1 *Tillandsia balbisiana* has sixteen-inch twisting leaves arising from a bulbous base. They are a light green with powdery scales. The inflorescence consists of a twelve-inch reddish-brown spike with vibrant purple flowers.

2 *T. circinnata* sends eight-inch, gray-green, twisted leaves from a bulbous base. The scale is a powdery-gray. Flowers have lavender petals coming from a pinkish spike.

3 *T. fasciculata* has gray-green leaves that will grow up to forty inches. My plant now averages

X1/2

twelve inches. Leaves are tapered and average two inches in width. The flowers have violet petals on brilliant red bracts.

4 *T. ionantha* has dense clusters of three-inch leaves, light green and covered with silvery scales. When the plant prepares to flower, all the leaves turn a rosy red. Tubular flowers have purple petals. This plant originates in Mexico.

5 *T. pruinosa* is a small plant that looks like a green plush octopus standing on its head. The leaves are three to four inches long, the total plant topping five inches. Flowers are rosy pink bracts with purple petals.

6 *T. setacea* resemble tufts of pine needles up to ten inches in length. Color is dark green in the shade but turning reddish brown with increased light. Flowers are purple on a pinkish stalk.

7 *T. valenzuelana* has a rosette of light-green leaves with silvery scales growing to twenty inches. Flowers have lilac petals with pink bracts on a curved, eighteen-inch spike.

Probably the most common member of the tillandsia family in America is the old southern favorite, Spanish moss (*T. usneoides*). From a distance it resembles hanging lichens or moss, but if you look closely you'll see one-inch leaves on threadlike stems and countless silvery scales. Tiny single flowers with chartreuse or blue petals appear on short stalks coming from leaf axils. I was told it would do well hanging on a wire in a sunny window, but would need daily misting. I tried it, but forgot our cold winter nights and it froze to death one January.

The next illustration shows five bromeliads growing on a piece of forest driftwood, anchored in a six-inch clay pot with osmunda, the surface covered with white gravel. This tree goes outside in summer, shaded from the noonday sun. The Dyckia and Cryptanthus (see below) are planted at the base because of their terrestrial nature. Others are wrapped in balls of osmunda and tied to the wood with nylon thread. Bring it inside before frost and handle just like the tillandsia log.

1 *Billbergia pyramidalis* grows as an epiphyte or a terrestrial. The plant shown is young, leaves are less than a foot long. As it grows older, leaves will reach two feet with a two-and-one-

half inch width. Color is light green with slightly darker stripes running lengthwise. The inflorescence grows from the center, with red bracts and red flowers. If misted properly, the cup will always be full of water.

2 *Neoregelia marmorata* has pale green leaves up to twelve inches long and two inches wide, marbled with reddish brown. The leaf tips are a brilliant red, hence the common name of fingernail plant. The color is reminiscent of fingernail polish during the Second World War. The inflorescence nestles in the vase of the plant. Petals are pale lavender.

3 *Orthophytum saxicola* is a small plant, rarely exceeding five inches in diameter. Leaves are bronze in color, edged with soft spines. My plant is bright green so I assume it is the variety *viridis.* Flowers are white.

4 *Dyckia encholirioides* (also known as *D. altissima*) is a rosette of bright green leaves edged with spines. Leaves grow up to eighteen inches, but mine is a young plant. The undersides of the leaf are finely traced with silvery gray pencil-like lines. Flowers are orange on a two-foot spike. This is a terrestrial plant so I planted it on the surface, but I'm sure it would do well wrapped in osmunda and tied higher in the tree.

5 *Cryptanthus bivittatus* is a member of an interesting group of terrestrial bromeliads. Their common name is earthstar. My plant has six-inch leaves with piecrust edges. Leaf colors are pink, the edges separated with a band of pale green. The undersides are reddish brown.

The following are plant descriptions of three more earthstars. The smaller types are excellent for terrariums.

Miniature red earthstar (*C. acaulis ruber*) has a three-inch rosette of green leaves turning to purple bronze at the center.

C. lacerdae is a small rosette of dark green leaves with silver borders and a broad, pale center band.

C. zonatus is commonly called the zebra plant. Brownish green leaves mottled with irregular bands of tan, form a twelve-to-fourteen-inch rosette.

X1/2

PROPAGATION OF BROMELIADS

After flowering, most bromeliads will die, but not before they send up offshoots which are easily rooted for new plants.

The common pineapple fruit will produce a handsome house plant. Cut off the top growth, taking about an inch of fruit. Let the cut air-dry a few days, then root in moist sand or peat moss. Move to a five-inch pot of peat moss when roots develop.

Bromeliad seeds will germinate on a bed of moist and warm sphagnum moss if the seed is fresh. To obtain seed, you'll have to do the job of pollenator. Since the individual flowers last but a day, upon opening remove an anther with a tweezers and let the pollen air-dry. By mid-morning, the stigma will be sticky. Apply the pollen with a Q-Tip or camel-hair brush. Some bromeliads are self-sterile so it's best to use two plants. I've only tried it with Billbergia, but the process worked.

ORCHIDS

My first introduction to the orchid was the purchase of a large, convoluted lavender flower with a twisted mass of grosgrain ribbon and an expensive price tag. My date at the high-school prom was properly thrilled. I was rather disappointed in the corsage and thought that field daisies were more attractive. Obviously none of the other girls at the dance had any love for daisies or the taste for that ostentatious flower of elegance would have died years ago. For the next decade, I thought all orchids looked like door prizes at a second-rate night club.

After an utterly drab two years in the army, I became fascinated with growing plants and saw my first orchid collection. I was amazed to learn that the orchid corsage was but one species of one genus out of eight hundred. I haven't changed my feelings on that one species (a Cattleya hybrid) but the rest are truly magnificent.

Here are three orchids that are inexpensive to buy (all under five dollars), easy to grow with minimum upkeep, and will flower every year.

Fiery Reed Orchid

Three years ago this July, I received a six-inch cutting of the fiery reed orchid from my garden friend in Florida. It now has three six-foot stems with three more on the way. Two stems have been in continual bloom since last November and show no signs of stopping. This orchid is a member of the epidendrum genus and is called *Epidendrum radicans* in the horticultural trade and *E. ibaguense* by botanists. In Florida backyards it can reach ten feet or more in height but doesn't start blooming until at least three feet high. About twelve one-inch scarlet flowers with fringed yellow lips are in bloom at one time—a globular mass of color.

The plant is potted in a six-inch pot with pure osmunda fiber that is never allowed to dry out completely, as these plants like continual moisture at the roots. Fertilizer is not used, as osmunda contains enough organic nutrients for at least two years of growth. In winter this orchid needs full sun. In summer, partial shade during midday. The stems need some support and bamboo stakes or a trellis should be provided. If reasonably happy, epidendrums will send up new shoots and the plants can be divided. Temperatures can fluctuate from a low of 45°F. in the winter to a high of whatever summer brings, as long as the plants are not baked to death in a closed room with full sun.

When humidity is low a daily misting is appreciated by the plant. It also likes clean leaves, so if you live in the city, wash the leaves every other week.

Pleione formasana

This is a charming terrestrial orchid from the mountains of Taiwan. Its cultural demands are small and, in return for the most basic of care it blooms every spring. Four-inch flowers of a rosy-lilac hue with a white fringed lip stand on four-inch stems. The interior of the lip is spotted with brown. The flowers last about two weeks, with cooler temperatures (50-60°F.); less if warmer. After the flowers fade, eight-inch pleated leaves appear for the summer.

I use the standard potting mix with some additional sand and extra crocking at the pot bottom. They should not dry out completely while in active growth, but you can forget to water occasionally without dire results. When the leaves die in early fall, withhold water and allow a winter rest. Begin watering in early spring.

Pleione prefers filtered sunlight. Direct summer sun will burn the leaves. Temperatures during winter should average 50°F. (just don't let the dormant plant freeze). In summer keep the

Fiery Reed Orchid
Epidendrum ibaguense

X 1

temperature as close to 70°F. as you can. During really hot weather, mist the leaves and try to keep a constant movement of air.

Seasons can be reversed as long as the other conditions remain the same and Pleione will flower in the winter and rest during the summer.

Butterfly Orchid

The common name of butterfly orchid or dancing doll is very apt. The flower sprays are long and drooping, swaying with every movement of air. The petals are yellow with sepals dotted with reddish brown. Flowers last a long time and make beautiful corsages and boutonnieres.

Of easy culture, this orchid does best as a hanging plant since it's epiphytic in the wild. Place it in a six-inch pot of pure osmunda and water liberally while in active summer growth. The leaves are thick, indicating a tolerance for short periods of drought; if you forget to water at times, it will not kill the plant.

Each spring after flowering, a new leaf begins next to the previous year's growth. It usually reaches a foot in length by the summer's end. Cut back on watering during the winter, about three times a month. Temperature should be cool—45°F. nights will do no harm, but the average nighttime temperature should be about 55°F., daytime 65-70°F. These orchids are very adaptable and you don't have to run about the house with a thermometer every day. Just try to prevent extreme and sudden changes in interior climate. Roots will shoot out in all directions, and a daily misting during the summer is very beneficial.

Repot every two to three years, when the osmunda fiber breaks down and becomes mushy. After a leaf is about five years old, it will yellow and die. Just cut it off near the plant base with a sharp, clean knife.

Propagate by dividing the plant, giving each new plant at least three leaves.

Other Orchids to Try

Listed in the Bibliography are a few excellent books on orchid culture for any who want to expand their orchid horizons—the only limitation being space and pocketbook. Many of the more common types will retail for under ten dollars, but the rarer hybrids and botanical orchids are very expensive.

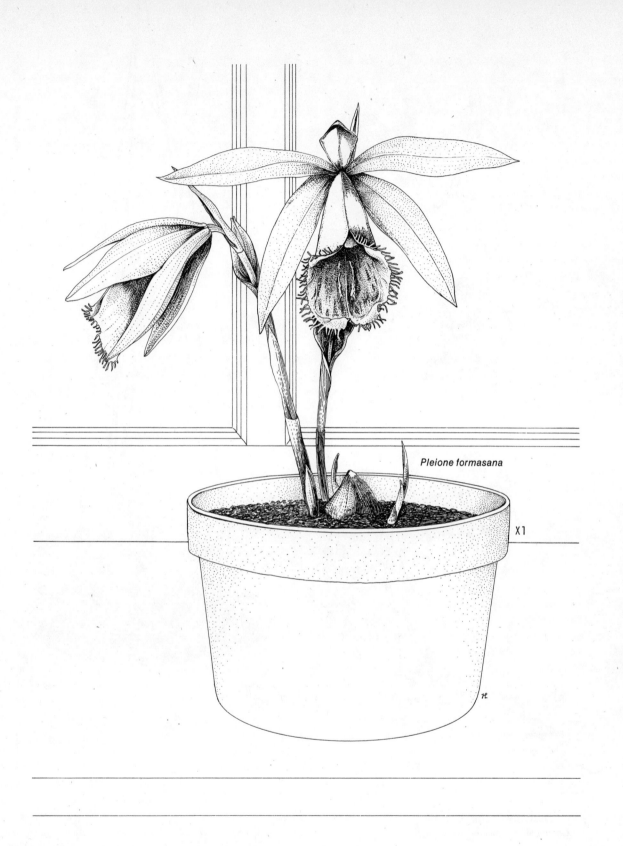

Pleione formasana

X1

X1

Butterfly Orchid
Oncidium cavendishianum

X1/2

CHAPTER ELEVEN
Wild Flowers

As far as I'm concerned the months of February and March are the worst part of the year in the Northeast—it seems winter has gone on for an indeterminable length of time and spring is either six months away or, possibly, delayed for a year. Forcing bulbs helps to brighten up the inside world, but wild flowers, with their small and bright blossoms, bring all the beauty of the deep woods to your indoor garden.

Growing and flowering wild flowers in the home is not at all difficult but there is one stipulation: you must have the facilities to winter the plants at an average temperature of about 45°F. in order that the plants have a dormant period. There are different ways of solving this problem. Build an indoor greenhouse, as described in Chapter Two—by adjusting the window, you can maintain lower temperatures without adversely affecting your living conditions. Or, if you have an area where you can dig a trench, you can winter the pots in the outside garden, while providing the needed dip in temperature but protecting the soil in and about the pots from freezing. (Frozen soil will not hurt the plants, but you'll need dynamite to dig them up in February and bring them inside.) Or you could use the far

recesses of the cellar, the back corners of the garage, or, as I do, the floor on the north side of the sun porch; or use a cool room and place the pots near a window, where the temperature will be much colder than the center of the room. If wild flowers are not allowed a dormant period in winter, they will not flower, and will provide a very depressing sight in the spring.

There are three ways to acquire the plants:

1 Dig them up from the woods and fields in the fall and pot them, once again asking permission from land owners and following state conservation laws.

2 Grow the plants from seed, remembering that only the dedicated can cope with seed propagation, since many wild flowers take years to reach maturity. The trillium, for example, will take three years to reach flowering size.

3 Buy established plants from wild flower nurseries (see Chapter 16). This is generally your best bet, as you are purchasing established plants, grown under cultivated conditions.

GENERAL RULES

Whether collecting from the field or buying plants, start the process in the fall. I send for stock in October, so the plants are all potted and settled by the first of November.

Unless they have unusual soil requirements, I use the standard potting mix, but I increase the amount of sand by at least 25 percent. Most of these flowers like moist and airy soil and dislike mud. Pot sizes vary from three to six inches, depending on the root mass, bulb size, or number of plants in a pot. I label each pot with its Latin and common name, its time of planting, and its source.

The soil is soaked and allowed to drain. The surface is mulched with sphagnum, vermiculite or perlite, for two reasons: to keep the soil from drying out too quickly and to cut off light. If the soil does start to dry out, the plants are rewatered.

About the middle of November, the pots are placed in plastic bags, tied tight, and moved to their winter quarters until February. If you don't use plastic bags, you'll have to check the soil all winter long as it should never become bone dry. In northern woods, these plants freeze in the ground all winter and cease activity. However, freezing cold is not necessary to insure dormancy

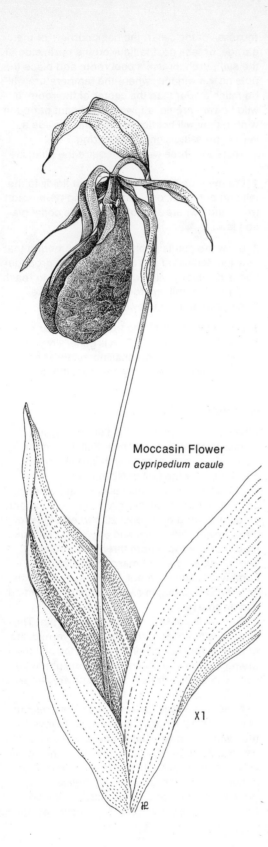

Moccasin Flower
Cypripedium acaule

X1

—45°F. works perfectly well. On the other hand, if the soil becomes bone dry the roots suffer damage, often permanently.

Around the end of February, take the pots out of the bags, remove the mulch, and place in a bright room at 50°-55°F. (a 65°F. room is usually that cold near a window) for about three or four weeks. As buds appear move to a sunny and cool window.

After blooming, continue watering and when the weather is good move the plants to the outside garden. I've never forced these flowers more than once. It may be possible, but by planting them outside, you increase the wild flowers in your garden and have room indoors to try new varieties.

I cannot guarantee the scientific accuracy of my approach, but it does work.

The illustrations are all from pot-grown flowers that bloomed from late February to April.

WILD FLOWERS TO FORCE

Moccasin Flower

One of our most beautiful wild orchids, the moccasin flower (*Cypripedium acaule*) is found in moist and acid soil, usually under pines throughout the Northeast and farther south in the mountains. Use an acid potting medium. I use 1/4 sand, 1/4 compost, and 1/2 peat moss. The bulb is planted under an inch of soil, and I add a mulch of pine needles. This year I intend growing the yellow lady's slipper (*C. calceolus*) and the showy lady's slipper (*C. reginae*).

It's interesting to note that these orchids live in conjunction with a soil fungus, so if digging them up yourself, take enough soil to completely surround the roots.

Spring Beauty

Spring beauty (*Claytonia virginica*) has white flowers with pink veins, or pinkish flowers with darker veins, which bloom in May in rich, moist woodland. It's a beautiful harbinger of spring. Blossoms open one at a time, but each plant has many buds. They close at night or in heavy shade.

Bloodroot

Growing from a thick rootstock, bloodroot (*Sanguinaria canadensis*) sends up a showy, solitary white flower up to an inch and one-quarter in diameter. If a stem is broken, it oozes a bright orange sap, used by the Indians of North America as a dye.

Hepatica

Two species of hepatica are found growing from southern Canada south to Georgia. The sharp-lobed (*Hepatica acutiloba*) and the round-lobed (*H. americana*). The leaves are liver-shaped and were once believed to be cures for diseases of this organ. The flowers are in shades of blue, white, pink, or lilac. A pot of these plants is a beautiful sight.

Because they grow in warmer parts of the United States, besides the Northeast, they can be brought into flower after a shorter dormancy. Bring them into a warmer room around January. It's worked for me two out of three tries.

Trillium

A study in threes, the trillium (*Trillium* spp.) has three petals, three sepals, and three leaves. The largest and showiest is the large white trillium (*T. grandiflorum*), often grown in northern gardens on the east and west coasts. Others are:

• Purple trillium (*T. erectum*) grows nine to eighteen inches high with a single purplish-red flower.

• Yellow trillium (*T. luteum*) has lemon-yellow flowers with a faint perfume and leaves of dark green with light-green splotches.

• Painted trillium (*T. undulatum*) has white flowers, petals streaked with pink or red at their base.

The decoration for the chapter title is a stylized painted trillium.

Foamflower

Foamflower (*Tiarella cordifolia*) is notable for both leaves and flowers. A six- to twelve-inch stem bears a raceme of tiny white flowers with ten long stamens. From a short distance the effect is a pillar of foam. The leaves are heart-shaped and sharply lobed with a fresh green color, showing darkish spots in good light. After the flowers have faded, the leaves make a very attractive pot plant, staying green well into the fall. This plant likes evenly moist soil so I use a self-watering pot.

X1

Spring Beauty
Claytonia virginica

Texas Sage
Salvia coccinea

X 3/4

Wild Ginger

These plants are grown for the evergreen foliage, not the flower, which hides at the base of the plant on the soil surface. The flower resembles a tiny brown bottle with three turned-back petals glued on the lip. The shiny green leaves are three to four inches long on three-inch stems. The northern species (*Asarum canadense*) is not evergreen and I have not grown it. It is interesting to note that the rootstock has a ginger-like odor and flavor and was used as a substitute for the real thing in days gone by. (Real ginger is not related, but is a tropical plant —*Zingiber zerumbet*—available as a rootstock in Chinese vegetable stores. It will root in a warm, moist soil.) *A. virginicum* and *A. shuttleworthii* are the two evergreen species for growing in pots.

Bleeding Heart

A perennial favorite in wild-flower gardens bleeding heart (*Dicentra eximia*) grows up to sixteen inches in height, bearing heart-shaped pinkish-red blossoms with a tiny "drop of blood" at the tip. Leaves are fresh green and fern-like. This plant is the wild version of the popular garden plant from Asia.

Another member of the family is the Dutchman's breeches (*D cucullaria*). with white blossoms that strongly resemble a pair of pantaloons hung upside down.

Both these plants force easily.

Texas Sage

Texas sage (*Salvia coccinea*) will reach a height of two feet with many vibrant red blossoms. Use the standard mix and let it dry slightly between waterings. This plant will grow and bloom most of the year so it doesn't need forcing procedures. Just grant it a rest by reducing water when flowering ceases, and no growth will be evident. This is the only red-flowered species found in North America. It's sold as a house plant or found growing wild in sandy soil from Florida to Texas on the coastal plain. Texas sage probably originated in Brazil.

Lungwort

Lungwort (*Pulmonaria saccarata*) is often confused with our native American wild flower, Virginia bluebell (*Mertensia virginica*) because of a

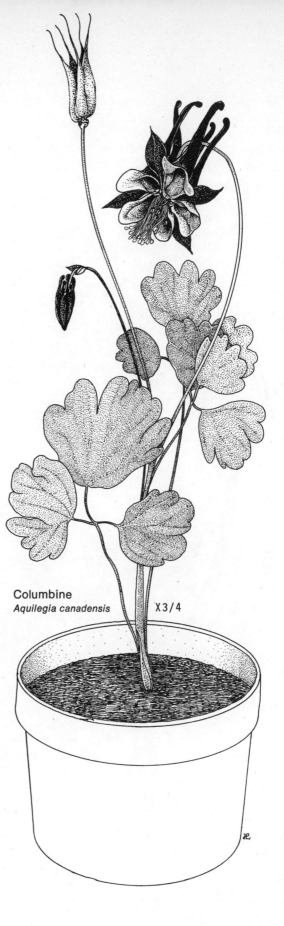

Columbine
Aquilegia canadensis   X 3/4

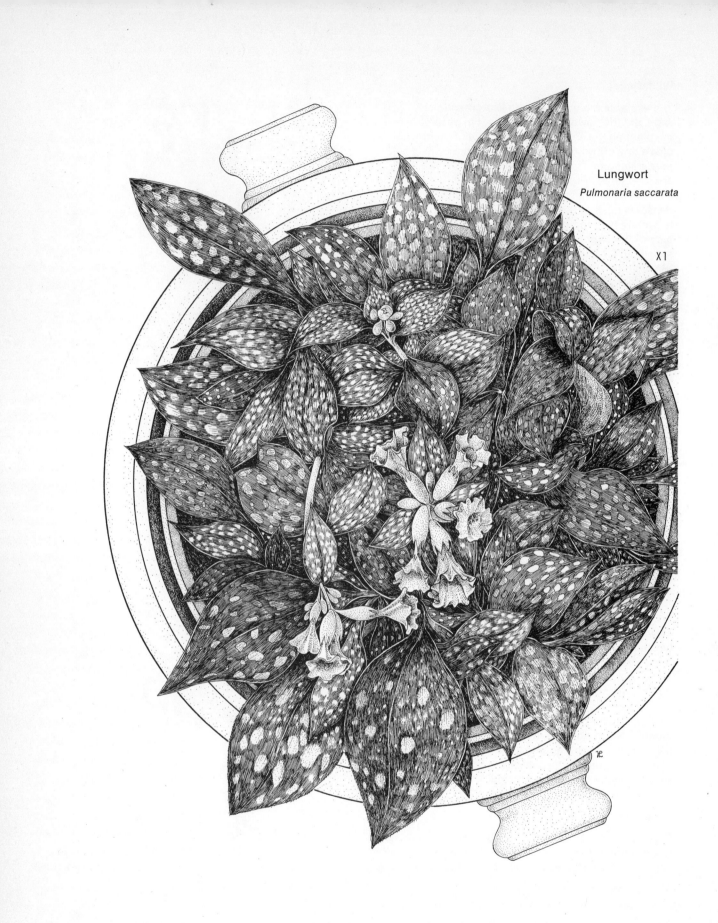

Lungwort
Pulmonaria saccarata

X1

great similarity between the flowers. Both have pink buds that turn blue as they open and both belong to the borage family, but the similarity ends there. Pulmonaria is a southern European plant with dark-green leaves, covered with tiny silver hairs and blotched with silvery-white spots. The common name is related to the lung-like appearance of the leaf, which was once thought to cure diseases of that organ.

Primarily a garden flower of long standing, it has escaped from cultivation and, since it's hardy, is now found growing wild in the eastern part of the United States.

The Virginia bluebell will flower when forced, like other wild flowers, but I've never tried it, as the leaves of lungwort are attractive without flowers.

Columbine

Wild columbine (*Aquilegia canadensis*) grows throughout eastern America south of Canada. Leaves are a soft green with lobed edges. The flowers are large and reddish-orange with yellow insides. Use the standard soil mix. They like the soil to dry out slightly between waterings.

The European columbine (*A. vulgaris*) has escaped cultivation and is often found growing wild in the same general area. The blossoms are blue, purple, pink, or white. The European variety has been widely hybridized to produce the large showy flowers of formal gardens, and these too may be forced for early bloom.

WILD FLOWERS FOR TERRARIUMS

The following flowers are smaller in habit than the previous plants, doing well in small pots but equally suited for culture in a glass-enclosed woodland garden.

Bluets

Whether you call these flowers bluets or quaker ladies (*Houstonia caerulea*), it's difficult to ignore their existence when driving through the northeast countryside in May and June. The flowers form dense carpets of blue along roadsides, in fields, and on lawns. The petals are a delicate blue fading to white, varying from plant to plant. A bright yellow center appears to have been drawn with a heavily laden paintbrush. Leaves are tiny and insignificant, hidden among the accompanying grasses. When placed in a

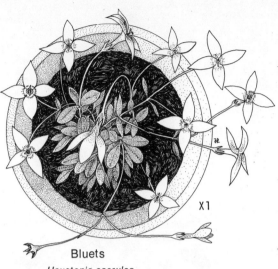

Bluets
Houstonia caerulea

cool terrarium for the winter, they burst into bloom in early March as the days become longer. They prefer evenly moist soil and when potting a bunch use a low dish rather than the typical pot.

Partridgeberry

Partridgeberry (*Mitchella repens*) is an evergreen plant of creeping habit with half-inch heart-shaped leaves of glossy green. It roots at nodes and eventually forms a dense mat of green. Twin flowers of pink or white, joined at the base, bloom in June and July. The plant grows in woods throughout the northeast. A single red berry is produced from the two flowers and if you examine it closely you can see two depressions at the tip of the berry which are the remains of the flowers. The berries are edible, with a spicy tang, and remain on the plant through winter until they're eaten by animals. The plant will grow easily in a pot or a bottle, but must be kept cool during the winter.

Wintergreen

Wintergreen (*Gaultheria procumbens*) has thick, shiny green leaves about an inch and one-half long that form an evergreen creeper. Small white flowers appear during July or August, followed by fragrant red berries. This plant is the source of wintergreen oil and is found in the northern United States.

Partridgeberry
Mitchella repens

X1

Crowberry

Crowberry (*Empetrum nigrum*) grows from the Arctic south to northern New York State. It's a low evergreen shrub, usually about six inches high. Tiny purple flowers bloom in June and July followed by black berries. This plant really favors moist and acid-peat soil.

Rattlesnake plantain

Rattlesnake plantain (*Goodyera pubescens*) has small evergreen leaves, veined with white and resembling snake-skin, which produce a six-inch stalk topped with a spike of tiny greenish-white orchids. Found in the northeastern United States in moist woods.

Gaywings

Called gaywings, fringed polygala, or flowering wintergreen (*Polygala paucifolia*), this is a delightful evergreen plant. The flowers resemble purple-pink orchids. The flaring wings are really sepals and two petals have united to form a tube, the lower one fringed. It blooms in May and June from southern Canada to northeast United States and south to the mountains in Georgia.

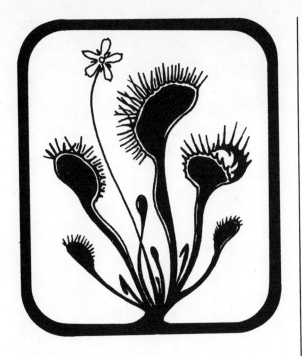

CHAPTER TWELVE
The Insectivorous Plants

There are over five hundred species of insectivorous plants found throughout the world, many in North America. They range in size from the microscopic fungi that loop themselves about an insect prey, quickly strangling it to death, to the impressive hanging pitcher plants of Borneo and New Guinea that not only ingest insects but an occasional mouse as well. This chapter deals with five distinct genera found within the continental limits of the United States. They can flourish indoors since junglelike temperatures are not necessary—nor do they need a diet of live food to survive.

Because these plants have poorly developed root systems and are generally found in wet and boggy conditions, high in acidity but deficient in nitrogens, they have developed the ability to fortify self-manufactured food supplies with an occasional relish of live meat. It has been definitely proved, with experiments on the sundew family, that this additional dash of organic nitrogen produces more vigorous plants with an increased capacity to flower and bear fruit. Insectivores can exist perfectly well without insects; they just produce fewer seeds. So *do not* give them

hunks of meat on an indiscriminate basis and *do not* fertilize with any plant foods; neither the leaves nor the roots are capable of handling this. My sister-in-law fed her Venus flytrap some kosher salami from a Brooklyn delicatessen one hot July, and the plant promptly expired. Perhaps the cause was lack of water, but it probably was the diet. These plants are engineered to take care of themselves, by choosing insects they can handle. If the prey is too large for the plant, either the prey or the plant withdraws, and the plant tries again for something smaller. If you give it hamburger, the plant begins with food that has long been deceased and the bacterial decay, already in process, can easily harm the plant.

Potting is a simple matter. Choose any container and put into it a layer of coarse gravel mixed with charcoal—at least an inch, and more, with a larger pot. Cover this gravel with a piece of plastic screening or osmunda or unmilled sphagnum to keep the soil from filtering to the bottom. Then add a layer of sterilized compost or soil, and top it off with sphagnum moss and/or peat moss. It's not absolutely mandatory to add the soil, but since I found out that most swamps have an underlayer of black organic matter with the improbable name of palms muck, I can't resist it. If you have access to live sphagnum, be sure to use it. As long as the moss stays green and healthy, the plants will do well. Finally, use rainwater or soft water, as these plants all require an extremely acid medium and will not adapt to hard water.

When planting a terrarium, give the growing medium a sloping effect and plant the pitcher plants down front, as they prefer to have their feet in water. The others like moist conditions but not sopping wet. If alone in pots, keep the pitcher plants in a saucer of water.

Along with a fondness for water, bog-loving plants prefer a high humidity level. The problem may be solved by using aquariums, fish bowls, gallon jugs with the narrow tops removed, bell jars, battery jars, kitchen glassware, and other combinations of glass and plastic. The tops should be partially covered but there must be adequate ventilation to prevent mold formations and allow for growth spurts and flowering.

Generally, I don't approve of terrariums with mixed genera even if the plants chosen have identical cultural demands. All plants grow and mature at different rates, which means endless rearranging and planting. If I do put more than one plant in a container, I always pot each one

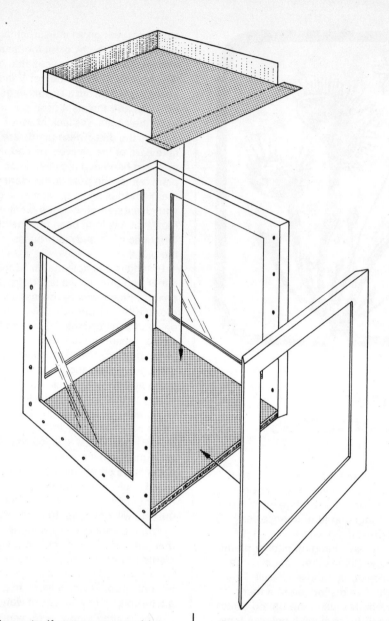

individually in clay pots. If one causes trouble with disease or disinterest, then it's easily removed without disturbing the others.

I foraged about locally and found five old window sashes from a remodeled house. By replacing the aged putty, beveling the edges with a Skil saw and screwing them together on a three-quarter-inch waterproof plywood base, I had an attractive and roomy "sweat box." The plywood was painted with a waterproof epoxy enamel and a plant trough made from folded aluminum sheeting. The pots were wrapped with sphagnum moss and the whole affair topped with the fifth window sash.

Swamps, contrary to horror films, are quite bright, as most large shade trees soon die in the water-logged conditions found there. As a result, these plants enjoy the sun. Since they're in closed containers, sweat boxes, or other enclosures to keep the humidity high, be careful to prevent heat build-up in the midday heat of summer. It's best to provide filtered sunlight at this time of day or the contents literally boil away.

Insectivores follow a yearly cycle of growth and generally go through a dormant period during the winter months. Don't despair as it's the natural thing for them to do. They'll soon send

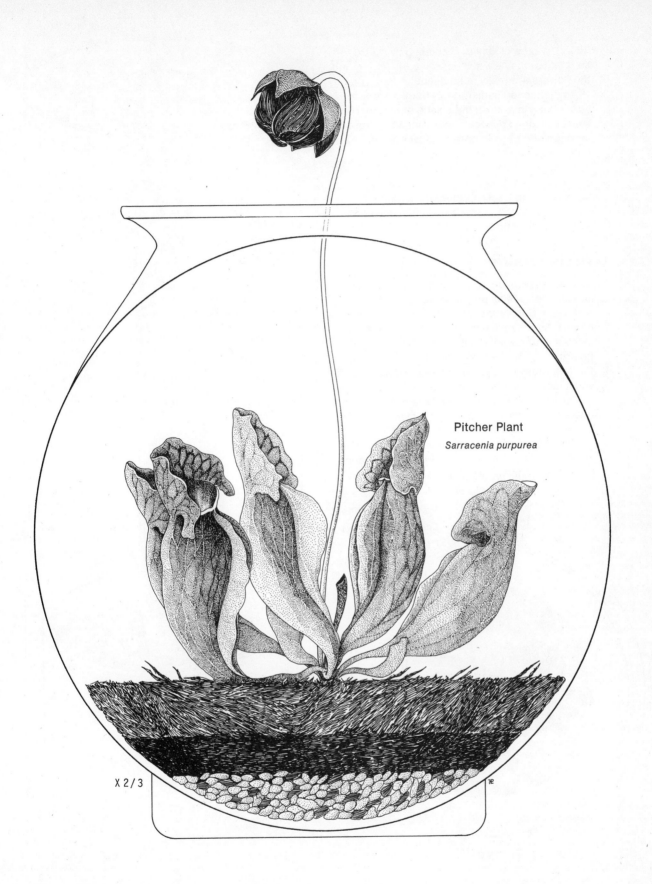

Pitcher Plant
Sarracenia purpurea

X 2 / 3

up a new crop of leaves. If conditions are to their liking, they will all flower in early spring and the flowers are really quite beautiful.

As mentioned earlier in this book, I'd like to add a few remarks on the pillage of natural resources. I don't advocate marching into virgin swamps and bogs to grab whatever tickles the fancy. However all over America, swamps and wetlands are continously being destroyed forever for a quick profit. When you see a bulldozer streaking in to level all before its path, try to salvage what's there, always asking first and complying with existing laws.

PITCHER PLANTS

The first insectivore to be carefully examined was the *Sarracenia purpurea*, found and described in North America by an unknown artist circa 1550. The plant itself was finally traced to Virginia and brought to England, alive, in 1640. Its bizarre shape and method of attaining insect food naturally caused quite a sensation in the scientific community of the times.

Nectar-producing glands on the outside of the pitcher send scent signals to the insect passing by. When the insect reaches the plant, it follows a honey trail leading to the pitcher's mouth. The fly or bug either slips over the edge or proceeds to the additional nectar glands which work in

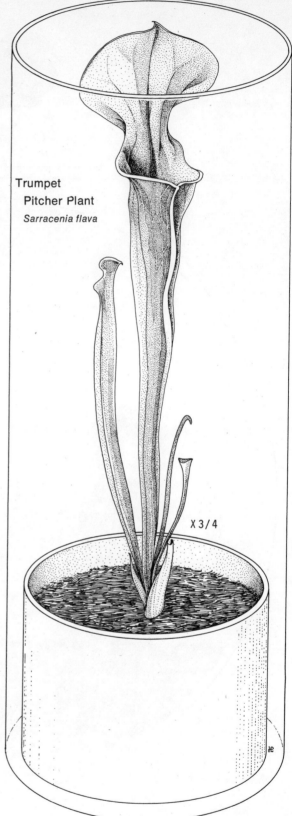

Trumpet
Pitcher Plant
Sarracenia flava

X 3 / 4

Parrot Pitcher Plant
Sarracenia psittacina

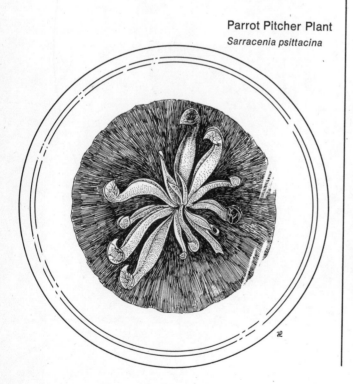

conjunction with glassy hairs pointing toward the bottom. It's very easy for the insect to walk and slide down the hairs, but they form an effective barrier when it tries to return to the top. Eventually the visitor drowns in the watery fluid in the base and is slowly digested by the plant's enzymes.

In nature, as in man, one always finds free-loaders and the pitcher plants are no exception. A small Canadian mosquito lays its eggs in the pitcher basin, where the larvae hatch and develop, immune to the plant's secretions. Frequently a spider will spin its web around the pitcher mouth, and interest an insect or two, before it even reaches the watery grave.

PLANT DESCRIPTIONS

The following are descriptions of eight species of pitcher plants found in North America. They do not bloom through the entire period indicated; generally, the warmer the environment, the earlier the plant blooms. Most are available commercially (see Chapter 16).

• Pitcher plant or sidesaddle flower (*Sarracenia purpurea*). The pitchers are lopsided and the lower curve rests on the ground. Leaves are in varying shades of green and purples and have pronounced veining. The flowers are a deep crimson, blooming from April to August. They are found throughout Canada and southward to Georgia and Louisiana in sphagnum and peat bogs. In the illustration, this species is housed in a two-gallon glass fishbowl from the five and dime.

• Parrot pitcher plant (*S. psittacina*) is limited to Florida, Louisiana, and Georgia, along the coast. It flowers from April to September with crimson petals. The pitchers are tube-shaped and lie flat upon the ground. This species is shown as a very young plant growing in decorative kitchen glassware.

• Sweet pitcher plant (*S. rubra*) flowers in April and May with red-purple blossoms that have a very sweet fragrance. The pitchers stand erect and are found in western Florida and extend to southern South Carolina.

• Fiddler's trumpet (*S. leucophylla*) stands erect with trumpet-shaped pitchers. The hood is white with red veining, and is similar in shape to *S. flava*. It blooms from April to September, with the typical crimson flower, and is found from northwest Florida to Mississippi and Georgia.

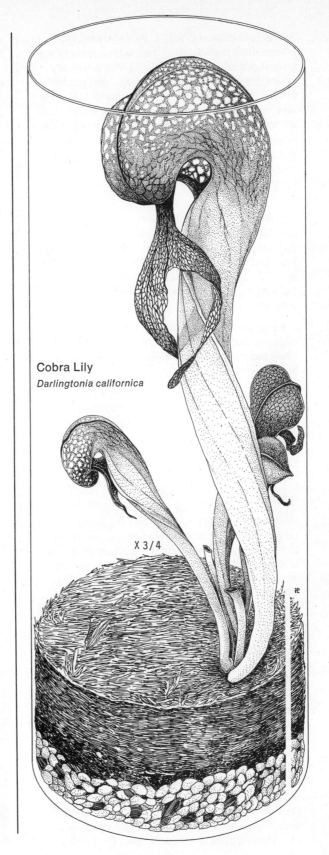

Cobra Lily
Darlingtonia californica

X 3/4

• Trumpet pitcher plant (*S. flava*) flowers from March to September with yellow blossoms in the typical pitcher-plant shape. The trumpets vary from light green to yellow. The trumpet pitcher plant is found from northern Florida to Alabama and Virginia. This species is pictured growing in a white ceramic pot, enclosed by an acrylic tube four-and-one-half inches in diameter and about one foot high. This plant will grow taller this year and the tubing can easily be replaced with a longer piece.

• Yellow trumpet (*S. alata*) has narrow trumpet-like leaves with a hood that almost covers the opening. The hoods show veining when younger, but may develop a yellowish cast with age. The flowers are greenish-yellow and bloom from April to July. It's found from Alabama to eastern Texas.

• Hooded pitcher plant (*S. minor*) has very small pitchers that are dwarfed by the yellow flowers. They bloom from April to May from Florida to North Carolina.

• *S. oreophila* is restricted to the mountains of Georgia and Alabama. In addition to the pitcher-shaped leaves, it produces a series of short, flat leaves. It flowers in May.

COBRA LILY

Discovered in 1841, in a marsh off a small tributary of the Upper Sacramento River, the Cobra Lily was immediately seen to be so distinctive as to warrant its own genus. It was dedicated and named after Dr. William Darlington of West Chester, Pennsylvania. According to botanical rules of nomenclature, it is properly called *Chrysamphora* but *Darlingtonia* still persists as the most frequently used name. It's found only in Oregon and northern California in the typical damp and boggy conditions enjoyed by most of the insectivores.

The dome is unusually firm and dotted with translucent windows, looking very much like a piece of Tiffany glass. The "beard" in front of the opening secretes nectar to draw unwary visitors. The pitcher is lined with stiff hairs that point toward the well below and these, in combination with additional nectar glands, lead an unsuspecting insect along the path to oblivion. Once in the water, there is no escape and the insect is drowned and digested by bacterial action. *Darlingtonia* is unique among the pitcher-type plants since they harbor active bacteria in their well that do the job of digestive fluids.

Be sure to provide a container large enough for these plants to grow up to two or three feet, since in an optimum home environment they could reach that height.

The *Darlingtonia* illustrated is growing in gravel, charcoal, soil and sphagnum, all placed in a one-foot battery jar.

BUTTERWORTS

There are at least five species of butterworts in the United States (four of which are described below). They consist of short vertical stems, scant roots, and a rosette of leaves that lie flat upon the ground. The leaves are pale green, shiny and greasy to the touch because of tiny glands that produce drops of organic mucilage over the leaf surface. The leaves are slightly rolled over at the edges and form natural wells for the digestion of small insects. Upon trapping additional food in the glue, the leaves will slowly roll over a bit more, but it's not an instantaneous reaction. It usually takes more than a day, but the glue works well and there is no place for the hapless victim to go.

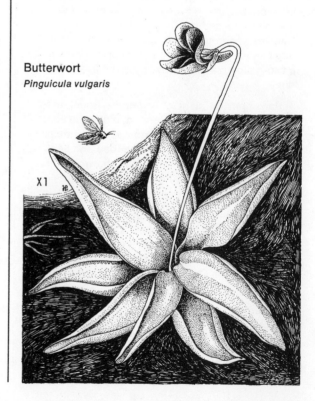

Butterwort
Pinguicula vulgaris

X1

Quite often, when growing bog plants in wet and moist sphagnum moss, you'll be attacked by fungus gnats. They're about the size of two printed m's close together. The gnats are just pesty, but the larvae feed on germinating seeds, plant roots, and decaying vegetation. Once started, you may expect a good many gnats. Butterworts are handy to have around as the gnats are just the right size to be caught and devoured.

PLANT DESCRIPTIONS

The common species of butterwort (*Pinguicula vulgaris*) is found in peat bogs and wet meadows in the northern part of the United States. Leaves about four inches long give rise to a beautiful violet-like flower on a six-inch stalk, which blooms in June or July. You'll find it across Canada, and south to Minnesota, Michigan, New York, and Vermont.

The following three American species are found farther south.

• Yellow butterwort (*P. lutea*) has yellow flowers often an inch or more across. It's found from Florida to Louisiana and North Carolina, and blooms from February to May.

• Violet butterwort (*P. caerulea*) has stems with violet flowers up to eight inches tall. It blooms from February to May on the coastal plain from Florida to North Carolina.

• *P. pumila* is the smallest of the butterworts. The leaf rosette is about an inch across. Solitary flowers are violet colored and borne on stems about four inches high. It blooms from February to July in moist, sandy soil from Florida to North Carolina and west to Texas.

SUNDEWS

The sundews are well represented by over ninety species found throughout the world. They vary in size from *Drosera gigantea*, an Australian species with forty-inch stems to our native sundew (*D. rotundifolia*), with its diminutive leaves, four-tenths of an inch in diameter.

During the nineteenth century, Charles Darwin was fascinated by the movements of these tiny plants and wrote a book on his findings that is still used today. He proved beyond a doubt their ability to catch, digest, and absorb insect meals, but did not prove to everyone's satisfaction that this ability is necessary to the plant's survival.

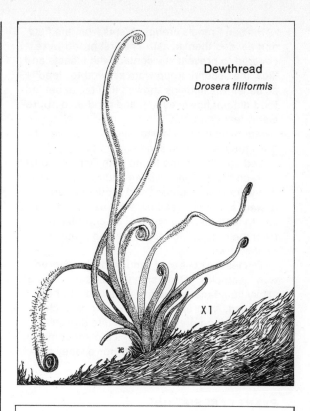

Dewthread
Drosera filiformis

X1

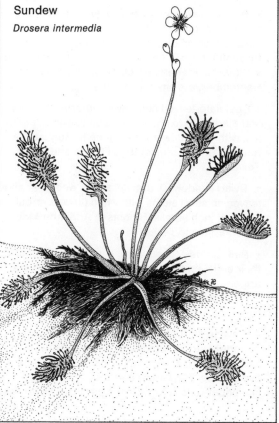

Sundew
Drosera intermedia

His son Francis brought plants from the field and divided them in half. The first group were covered to prevent any contact with insects and flies; the second group were allowed to "feed" as usual. His findings showed that those denied food did not flower as well and produced appreciably less seed.

Much criticism followed, and other scientists grew the plants from seed under strictly controlled conditions and found both Darwins to be correct: those plants with an additional insect diet were more vigorous and produced more flowers and more seeds. It's not necessary for you to feed them—if not shut off completely from the outside world, they will do pretty well on their own.

The leaves consist of reddish pads covered with "tentacles." Glands on the pads produce a sticky liquid that attracts insects and catches them fast. After an insect sticks, the tentacles bend over and press the victim into digestive juices. The common name of the plant comes from the sparkle of the glue drops as they glisten in the sun.

PLANT DESCRIPTIONS

• Round-leaved sundew (*Drosera rotundifolia*) is the most commonly found species and has circular leaves on distinct petioles. It's found throughout North America in spagnum bogs and wet places. Flowers, which bloom from June to September, are small and white.

• Spatulate-leaved sundew (*D. intermedia*) has leaf blades up to an inch long on two-inch petioles, with white flowers from June to August. It's found from Ontario south to Florida and west to Texas.

• Dwarf sundew (*D. brevifolia*) has wedge-shaped leaves on short stems with white flowers about one-half inch across. Blooms in April and May from Virginia to Texas.

• Pink sundew (*D. capillaris*) has leaves widest at their ends, on long, smooth stems. The flowers are one-third inch across, pink in color, and bloom from May to August. The plants are found from North Carolina to Florida and Texas.

• Dewthread (*D. filiformis*) has leaves like pieces of upright string, with no distinctions between leaf and stem. The glandular hairs cover the entire surface. They unwind as they grow, much like paper rolls at New Year's parties. The leaves grow up to ten inches, depending on their age and environment; the flowers are pink on nine-inch stems, and bloom from May to August. The southern plants are larger than their northern counterparts. The plants are widely distributed from eastern Massachusetts to the coast to Florida.

VENUS FLYTRAP
(*Dionaea muscipula*)

This is the best-known of all the insectivores, conjuring up images of giant vicious jaws snapping shut on hapless ladies in abbreviated sun-suits foraging the Amazon jungles for lost treasures or lost friends. While not a giant among plants (nor especially fond of undressed maidens) it's a most fascinating specimen. Found only in North and South Carolina in bogs, moist sandy areas, and wet pinelands, the Venus flytrap was discovered by a Governor of North Carolina in 1759. Governor Arthur Dobbs published the following description: ". . . But the great wonder of the vegetable kingdom is a very curious unknown species of sensitive; it is a dwarf plant . . . leaves are like a narrow segment of a sphere, consisting of two parts, like the cap of a spring purse, the concave part outward, each of which falls back with indented edges (like an iron spring fox trap); upon anything touching the leaves, or falling between them, they instantly close like a spring trap . . . it bears a white flower; to this surprising plant I have given the name of Flytrap Sensitive."

So far, I've not been able to find out who thought up the delightful term "Venus" but it was obviously an eighteenth-century misogynist.

The traps are green in poorer light and turn a deep crimson as the light increases. The surface of each trap has three hairs which respond to touch by closing the traps. The time needed to snap shut can be several seconds or less than one-half second, depending on the age of the traps and the temperature; the greater the heat the faster the traps can close. They will usually reopen within a day if fooled by a broomstraw, matchstick or other object used to demonstrate the plant's unusual abilities. If it does catch a meal, it's digested in four to twenty days, depending on the size of the victim. The signal hairs must be touched twice within about twenty seconds or they will not close, probably to prove to the leaf that it has a live catch and not just a leaf. After a few meals or due to increasing age,

Venus Flytrap Plant
Dionaea muscipula

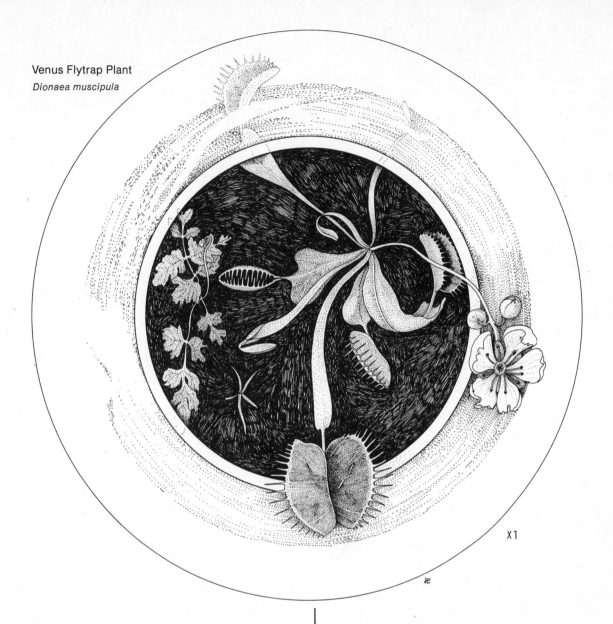

X 1

the traps turn black, so snip them off and new traps will grow.

Like all the others, the Venus flytrap likes lots of sunshine and high humidity. The roots do not like to sit in water but require constant moist surroundings. It's best to water a bit every day with warm and soft water.

Mature plants can have up to twelve traps at the same time under ideal conditions, and may be moved outdoors during the summer in a sunny and moist spot, to be brought inside when temperatures start to drop below 60°F., on a seasonal basis.

In late spring, the plant produces small, whitish flowers, with wavy edges, that are very dainty and attractive.

If the environment gets very cold, or extremely dry, the bulb enters a dormant period of about two months. This is the normal yearly cycle.

Don't be disappointed in the size of many traps. New plants grow smaller traps than established and more mature plants. When buying bulbs, they are graded as to age, not size.

CHAPTER THIRTEEN
Bulbs for Year-round Bloom

The introduction of the plastic bag has not been a great event in terms of cultural advancement, but it's a boon for the person who wants to force bulbs and is short on time and space. Before "Baggies," pots had to be buried outdoors in cold frames or, if started indoors, watered every few days. Once started, bulbs should not be allowed to dry out and if you forgot your charges for a week, they usually died.

The only requirement for forcing a bulb is a cool room, garage, or cellar that maintains a temperature of 45°-50°F. With the present energy crisis and the high cost of fuel, this temperature range should not be too difficult to maintain.

The procedure is as follows: Use six-inch *used* clay pots. New clay pots will not work! I don't know the reason but it's good advice based on generations of experience. Plastic pots are all right, but roots really benefit from the exchange of air through the porous walls of clay. Plan on three to six bulbs per pot. The medium should be a mixture of one-half peat moss and one-half vermiculite. Allow plenty of room

for the mixing and potting, and keep a vacuum cleaner handy.

Take a pot, crock the drain hole, fill about two-thirds with the mix. Tamp it down. Set the bulbs carefully on the medium about an inch apart. Don't twist the bulbs. The bulb bottom can easily be damaged and embryo roots destroyed. Fill the spaces around the bulbs, leaving the noses uncovered.

Now you're ready for the soaking operation. If you have more than a few pots, commandeer the bathtub. The pots must be soaked for twenty-four hours. (As you immerse each pot, hold your hand over the top. If you don't, the dry mix will float right out and you'll have a mess.) After soaking, drain the pots for another twenty-four hours. It won't hurt to cut the draining and soaking times by a few hours; the important point is to get the mix wet, but not dripping.

Take each pot and put it into a plastic "Baggie," tie the top and move to a cold and dark place for eight to twelve weeks. We have a work room that is partially heated and maintains an average temperature of 50°F. By putting pots near a window and covering them with layers of newspaper to keep out *all* light, the temperature averages about 45°F.

Bulbs will not bloom without a completely developed root system. Since conditions vary, check pots at the end of eight weeks. If roots are peeping through the drainage hole, pots are ready for the next step.

Remove the plastic bags and move pots to a bright place with a temperature of 50°-55°F. for about a week to ten days. Keep the pots from direct sun. When leaves are four to six inches high, move to a sunny window for blooming. After blossoms start to open, they'll last longer if moved from direct sunlight. Never let the medium dry out.

After the flowers fade, cut them off close to the bulbs, keep watering and allow the leaves to mature and die naturally. Then transplant to the garden for future blooming.

Quality bulbs contain all the nutrients necessary to grow and flower without soil or fertilizer. The embryo flowers have formed by the August before planting. While bulbs cannot be forced a second time because the very act of growing in this fashion prevents their building up reserves for the following year, many will regain enough strength, after a year or two of rest, to bloom in the spring garden. Occasionally one hears stories about blooming the following year, but it's a rare happening.

Star of Bethlehem
Ornithogalum umbellatum

X1

Hyacinth for Christmas

To have hyacinths for Christmas display, start potting about September 20 using *prepared* bulbs. These bulbs have been subjected to a pre-cooling period of 41°-48°F. during August and September by the grower. "Forcing" bulbs is a poor choice of words. They all need definite periods of cold in order to bloom. All you are doing is moving up the timetable.

Many bulbs have traveled from Europe in closed containers, and like all living things, need air. Bulbs should be opened for ventilation when you receive them. If you cannot plant immediately, poke holes in the paper storage bags and keep at a temperature below 68°F.

The following hyacinth cultivars are usually offered as prepared bulbs:

Anna Marie: clear pink
Madame Kruger: pure white
Delft Blue: blue
Jan Bos: scarlet

Other Hardy Bulbs

Daffodils are easy bulbs for indoor cultivation and this includes narcissus. Many people are confused about the difference between the two. The word daffodil refers to flowers belonging to the genus *Narcissus* which produce a trumpet on the flower. The best varieties to use are the early bloomers as:

Beersheba: white trumpet
Rembrandt: yellow trumpet

Tulips are reputed to be chancy flowers to force. I've only tried one variety, an early spring bloomer, Red emperor (*Tulipa fosteriana*), and had complete success. When planting these bulbs use about six to a pot and place the flat side toward the edge of the pot, since this is the direction the first leaf will take, growing gracefully over the edge instead of toward the center.

Spring-flowering crocus, grape hyacinths, star of Bethlehem, and *Iris reticulata* are all easy plants to bloom in winter. Just remember to give adequate time for rooting and keep records for future tries. The following table gives the average times for the initial cold period.

Spring-flowering crocus	4 weeks
Ornithogalum	8 weeks
Iris reticulata	8 weeks

Hyacinths	12 weeks
Narcissi	12 weeks
Tulips	14 weeks

Spring Bulbs for Flower Arrangements

One of the most effective floral centerpieces I've ever seen can be put together by digging up daffodils or tulips when they begin to bloom, carefully washing off the soil and filling battery jars with plants and water. The flowers last longer than if cut, but unfortunately the plants must be discarded when flowers fade.

Lifting Outdoor Bulbs

If you have bulbs planted in the outdoors, try the following for bringing a bit of color into the home. When dwarf iris, crocus, snowdrops, miniature daffodils, grape hyacinths and scillas push up through the soil, carefully dig them up with a garden fork, going as deep into the soil as you can. Pot them up, packing the bulb mix around them, and bring into a warm room. Water faithfully and they will generally bloom within two weeks. After blooming, and maturing the leaves, take this opportunity to divide the clumps and plant outside in autumn.

I've never tried this with the larger bulbs for fear of extensive damage to the root systems.

Lily-of-the-Valley

When ordering bulbs, remember to buy some prepared lily-of-the-valley (*Convallaria majalis*). They are available preplanted in a special mix and all you add is water. You can, however, save a bit of money and get more attractive containers by buying the pips and planting them yourself. They can be potted in almost any material that holds water, but your bulb mix is as good as any. The roots are planted in three-inch-high dishes, with the buds just above the surface. Water thoroughly and place them in a cardboard box with holes for ventilation. Keep about two weeks at room temperature. Then place the pots in a darkened area for a few days before exposing to bright light.

Tender Bulbs in Water

Every year, about September, tender bulbs of the narcissus family are offered for easy culture during the winter months. Paper-white narcissi,

Grape Hyacinth
Muscari armeniacum
'Heavenly Blue'

X 3 / 4

soleil d'or, and Chinese sacred lilies are the three varieties offered. They come preplanted or you may buy bulbs alone and pot them in your own containers. Use a bowl at least three inches high. Pebbles, gravel or the bulb mix will keep the bulbs stable. Fill the container with two inches of mix and add water till the mix is covered. Place the bulbs on top, gently, and surround the bulbs with more mix or stones to keep them upright, leaving the top half clear. Since these bulbs are preconditioned by the growers, they do not require intense cold. Place them in a cool (50°-60°F.), dark, well-ventilated spot until the leaves are about three inches tall. Move the pot to a lighted area for three or four days, then set the pot in the sun. Rotate containers occasionally so the leaves do not lean. Always keep the medium moist, but never let the bulbs themselves get wet, only their roots. You'll have to throw them out after blooming.

Water Culture of Hardy Bulbs

With the renewed interest in indoor gardening, I've noticed that the larger mail-order houses and many nurseries offer special glasses for growing hyacinths, crocus and other small hardy bulbs in water. A major Swedish glass firm gets

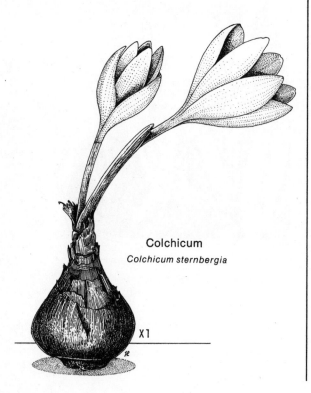

Colchicum
Colchicum sternbergia

X1

fifteen dollars for two crocus glasses and two corms, but this is an exception. Most glasses cost under three dollars.

You simply fill the glasses up to the neck with water and place the bulbs in the cup so just the base of the bulb touches water. Use rainwater or ordinary chlorinated tap water, which has been left to stand for a few days.

Hyacinths (both hardy and Roman), dwarf early-flowering tulips, grape hyacinths, and crocus may also be grown in the following manner:

The bulbs are covered with a paper hood and the containers placed in a dark, cool spot (45°-50°F.) for about ten weeks. Look at the glass at least once a week to check the water level and add more as needed. When the glass is full of roots and the leaves about two inches high move to about 55°F. for two weeks and then to normal room temperatures. The paper hood is removed when the bud emerges.

AUTUMN CROCUS

We generally associate crocus with early spring, but they have a lookalike, colchicum or autumn crocus, that belongs to the lily family. Crocus have three stamens, colchicum have six. You've never had an easier plant to bloom. When ordered in August, you can have them blooming in September merely by placing the bulbs on a sunny windowsill. After the bloom fades, plant outdoors with winter protection in the north. The leaves appear in the spring. This unusual plant also produces the drug colchicine. Discovered by the ancient Egyptians, it's been used as a specific for gout for centuries. Plant breeders found that it doubled chromosomes in cell nuclei producing many new hybrids, and today the drug has new applications in the treatment of an inherited disorder called familial mediterranean fever.

• *Colchicum autumnale* have two-inch flowers of soft rosy-lilac.

• *C. speciosum alba* produces a large, pure white flower.

STERNBERGIA

These are brilliant yellow flowers that bloom within a few weeks of potting. Although they bloom in autumn and look like crocus, they really belong to the amaryllis family. *Sternbergia*

Red Emperor Tulip
Tulipa fosteriana
'Red Emperor'

lutea is generally offered by nurseries. The leaves keep their color during the winter, and die back in spring.

ACIDANTHERA

Acidanthera are tender bulbs, growing from corms that bloom in September. The flowers are relatives of the gladiolus without the funereal quality of glads. *Acidanthera bicolor murieliae* have straplike leaves about eighteen inches long. The flowers, eight to twelve on a stem, are sweet-smelling and creamy-white with chocolate blotches at the center.

Plant the corms two inches deep and two inches apart in the standard mix during April. Start earlier in March if you have a heating cable for bottom warmth, and they'll bloom in late July.

Since they prefer full sun and evenly moist soil, I grow them in Riviera pots. They grow magnificently, as the corms get all the water they need.

After flowering, when foliage starts to die back, stop watering and store them directly in the dry pot at 55°-60°F. for the winter. Don't let the temperature go below 55°F. as the bulbs will suffer from the cold.

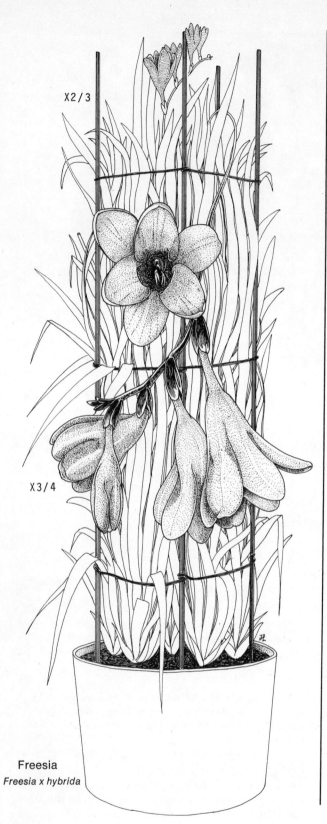

X2/3

X3/4

Freesia
Freesia x hybrida

If left in the pot, start watering in the spring and fertilize monthly when the leaves are well out of the soil.

Acidantheras form small cormlets around the basal plate of the corm. Plant them separately and they will develop flowers in two growing seasons.

LILY-OF-THE-NILE

Agapanthus africanus is a beautiful plant from South Africa. A tuberous root stock with very fleshy roots produces straplike, rich green leaves well over two feet long. Leaves are evergreen. In summer, two-foot stalks appear with terminal clusters or umbels of twenty or more pale blue flowers, each two inches long. They like full sun but will tolerate partial shade. Copious amounts of water must be supplied during the summer months and they flower best when rootbound. My plant is three years old and will soon crack its ten-inch clay pot. The next move will be a wooden tub. Fertilize once a month.

Agapanthus will grow all year round in the south, but up north bring it in for the winter before frost. Keep cool and moderately dry.

New plants appear at the base and the clumps may be divided. Plants may be grown from seed, but it takes about five years to reach flowering size.

Two additional species are available:

• *A. africanus alba*: the same plant with white flowers.

• *A. africanus* 'Peter Pan': A twenty-inch-high dwarf for small terraces. Flowers are blue.

LILIES

I owe a debt of gratitude to the Park Seed Company for introducing me to prepotted lilies for indoor winter bloom. In writing this book I was going to stay away from lilies because of a few bad experiences with indoor culture. Beautiful they may be, but up to now better outdoors. This experience has changed my mind.

I ordered a prepotted bulb in December, added water on arrival, and placed the pot in a south window shaded by a white pine from eleven to one o'clock. The growing medium was kept moist, not wet. Suggested temperatures were 70°-75°F. during the day and 60°-65°F. at night. Since my sun porch is on the chilly side, I moved the pot every evening into the kitchen. The stem grew to two feet, and at the end of March, six beautiful blooms appeared.

After the blossoms faded, they were cut off; the plant will continue to stay green until the foliage dies. After a rest period, I'll pot it up again in a mix of one part potting soil, one part peat moss, and one part sand. Fertilize once a month.

The three hybrids offered are:

Enchantment: nasturtium red
Harmony: rich orange
Cinnabar: glowing deep red

These bulbs are Asiatic hybrids developed by Mr. Jan de Graaf of lily fame.

Many lilies can be grown in pots for summer bloom, where they make a magnificent show on porch or terrace. I'm not going to give any instructions on this, but refer you to the Bibliography at the end of the book.

WATSONIA

Watsonia (*Watsonia humilis maculata*) are related to gladiolus but, like acidanthera, more attractive to me. Easy to grow and bloom, bulbs should be potted in a five- to six-inch pot in September. Later pottings yield later flowers. Soak and drain the mix and wrap in a plastic bag. Put the pot in a cool room (50°F.) for eight weeks or so, until roots are well developed. Then place in a sunny window and watch sword-shaped leaves develop up to three feet in length. Keep the mix evenly moist and feed the plant every three weeks. Mine bloomed in early May and the leaves made a great show all winter long. After the flowers fade, clip them off and reduce watering until the foliage yellows. Keep them dry and dormant for the summer and start again in the fall.

Propagate with the cormlets that form around the base of the mother corm. Plant separately for flowers in two growing seasons.

FREESIA

I was introduced to these lovely flowers by the grower in our local greenhouse. On a bleak February afternoon he was showing me their collection of growing Easter lilies when I noticed a rich, sweet aroma. We walked over to pots of tall

X 1

Watsonia

leaves and sprays of nodding waxy-yellow flowers. Most of the freesias had been cut for floral displays but the few that were left perfumed the greenhouse.

Easy to grow for winter bloom, the only requirement is a cool 50°-55°F. Plant eight corms in a six-inch pot of mixed peat moss and vermiculite. The corms should be about an inch below the level of the mix. Be careful to protect the husk that covers the surface. Water well and leave for about ten days. The pots need not be protected from light. The mix should be kept on the dry side, never wet. As the leaves develop, stake the plants with four bamboo canes and string (see illustration). The plants grow so tall that they will flop over if not held up. Give them maximum light for the best flower production. Use plant food monthly. They'll bloom in about four months.

After flowering, remove the dead flowers and withhold water while the foliage dies back. Put the pots aside and allow the corms to ripen for the summer and start again in fall.

MONTBRETIAS

South African members of the iris family, these sword-leaved plants produce ten to twenty bright orange flowers on two-foot stems during July and August. They last a long time as cut flowers and are striking as color accents when placed about the house in summer.

The corms are usually available in March and April and should be potted immediately. Plant four to five corms in a six-inch pot, one inch deep in the standard mix. Water once, then wait until growth starts before watering again. They need maximum light and prefer soil on the dry side. Stake them like freesias.

After flowering, withhold water as the leaves die. Leave in pots for the winter and start again in spring. They seem to bloom better when corms are crowded. Every two years repot and get new plants from the cormlets about the base of the mother corm.

The Latin name is *Crocosmia* x *Crocosmaeflora,* and hybrids are available in colors ranging from lemon-yellow to brilliant scarlet. They are also known as tritonia.

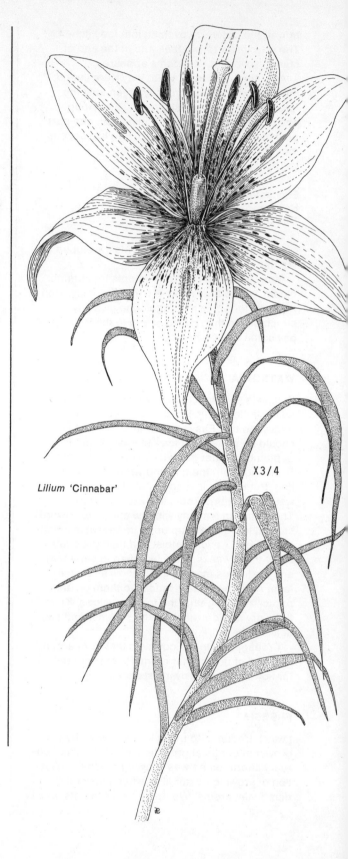

Lilium 'Cinnabar'

X 3/4

CHAPTER FOURTEEN
Old Favorites

This chapter deals with garden plants, gift plants for holidays and how to keep them all year, and a few favorite house plants of undemanding character for the person who thought nothing would ever grow.

GARDEN PLANTS FOR INDOOR BLOOM OR FOLIAGE

The following plants will do beautifully either in home or garden and can be changed at will.

Browallia

This is a favorite plant sold in many garden centers for summer gardens or patio containers. The lovely blue flowers have five petals on a long tube, growing profusely on a foot-high plant. Pot the plants in the standard mix in late August, giving the plants a few weeks to adapt to pot culture, before bringing indoors. Browallia (*Browallia speciosa*) can be freely pinched back to promote bushy growth and a new round of flowers. Give the plants partial shade in summer, but full sun in fall and winter, keeping the soil evenly moist. Grow from seed at any time.

Geraniums

These plants are considered by many to be un-excelled for cemeteries, unattended window boxes, and urban street displays. People never learn about the vast variety found in this family; they also never seem to learn that a little less July sun and a little more water produce more beautiful plants. Botanically called *Pelargonium*, they should not be confused with our native *Geranium* which are wild flowers, weeds, or garden perennials. I point this out to save you time when reading catalogs and indexes, since the listings for Geranium will invariably say: *see Pelargonium*.

There are four general groups: the show pelargonium (*P. domesticum*) of limited use in the home because of a short flowering season and a definite preference for cool temperatures; the zonal geranium (*P. hortorum*), so named because of the distinctive zones of color variation on the leaves; the ivy-leaved geranium (*P. peltatum*), and the scented-leaved geranium (*Pelargonium* spp.) which come in fifty or more species and almost as many variations in aroma. A fifth group comprises the "odd" geraniums, a group of different species resembling cactus and succulents.

Zonal geraniums are all hybrids of the original plant from South Africa and since there are well over 150 named hybrids, I doubt if anyone remembers what the original looked like. 'Olympic Red' and 'S.A. Nutt' are the popular denizens of Forest Lawn but zonals come in many more sizes and colors to match: orange, pink, salmon, apple blossom, white, near purple, and magenta.

Dig up the plants in the fall from garden beds, pot in the standard soil mix, generally with five- or six-inch pots. Remove all flowers, buds, and trim back some of the branches, shaping the plant. The stem cuttings you remove can be easily rooted (see Chapter 5). The mother plant should be placed in a cool room or window where it can get as much fall and winter sun as possible. The cuttings, when rooted, should be given the same exposure; pinch them back to promote bushiness and remove any buds that form until late spring. They'll bloom all summer, thus saving both time and money.

The mother plant will bloom all winter, producing less flowers than the previous summer, if given water when the soil becomes dry, plenty of winter sun, and cool (50°-60°F.) temperatures. In the spring, start removing any buds that form (you now have cuttings for summer bloom) and continue the process till fall. Now the original mother plant will reward you with lots of flowers and continue to grow; by following the same procedure each year you will eventually have a giant plant.

Never over-fertilize geraniums, since this will lead to a great many leaves but very few flowers. Wait six months after potting before giving plant food. Keep plants on the potbound side as they are more proficient bloomers. Occasionally geraniums will develop a stem rot, where the stems, especially those of cuttings, turn black. Cut away the infected parts and always use clean media for rooting cuttings. Overwatering will cause corky growths to appear on the leaves; cut down on water, remembering to water only when the soil becomes dry.

Ivy-leaved geraniums make great hanging-basket plants, preferring cool surroundings, some shade, and evenly moist soil. Otherwise treat the same as the zonals.

Scented-leaved geraniums have been grown on window sills for years. Their flowers are not as showy, but the leaves come in a variety of shapes and each species produces a unique scent, especially when you rub the leaves.

• *P. capitatum* has deeply lobed, light green leaves with a strong scent of roses. Flowers are orchid-pink.

• *P. crispum* has tiny, crinkled leaves with a strong scent of lemon. Flowers are pink with purple veining.

• *P. odoratissimum* is a trailing variety with moss-green, rounded leaves that smell of apples. The flowers are white.

• *P. tomentosum* has large-lobed, velvety leaves with a strong smell of peppermint. Flowers are white with feathery petals.

• *P. parviflorum* is a trailing plant with small round leaves that smell of coconut. Flowers are small and magenta.

The odd geraniums usually grow from tubers, are dormant during the summer months, sending up leaves and flowers for the winter.

• *P. dasycaulon* is a low-growing succulent plant with knobby branches and deeply cut fleshy leaves and small clusters of creamy-white flowers.

• *P. echinatum* has a succulent stem, producing soft, thorn-shaped stubble. Leaves are gray-green on top and white and hairy beneath. The flowers are single, white, and each petal is marked with a maroon spot of color.

Impatiens

A popular house and summer garden plant for generations, the impatiens plant (*Impatiens walleriana*) is also called the touch-me-not, since the seed pods burst upon the slightest provocation, scattering the seeds. They are simple to grow and available in a bewildering number of hybrids with colors of white, orange, salmon, purple, lavender, and red. New varieties appear on the market every year.

Lift up the plants in fall, pinch back (using the excess stems for cuttings), and give full winter sun, temperatures below 65°F., and keep the soil evenly moist. In summer, they prefer partial shade.

I now have a mother plant that is over four years old, and shows no signs of giving up. It's in a five-inch pot, and the bottom of the stem is now becoming calloused like a tiny tree trunk. Cuttings have been taken every year for the summer garden, all from an original fifty-cent investment.

Lavender

I've kept away from herbs in this book, but there is one that is a most delightful plant to have in the indoor garden.* You can buy a plant from a nursery and put it directly in a pot, or dig one up from an herb garden. Lavender (*Lavandula officinalis*) has squarish stems, covered with narrow gray-green leaves that yield the fragrance used for soaps and perfumes. In late summer, tall spikes of tiny, fragrant, blue flowers appear. Give the plant full sun all year, water when the soil becomes dry, use the standard mix, and keep the temperature around 60°-65°F. I move the pot outside for the summer every year. Don't fertilize, just repot every two years. Propagate by cuttings.

*Among the garden herbs that do well indoors are borage (*Borago officinallis*), lemon verbena (*Aloysia triphylla*), marjoram (*Majorana hortensis*), parsley (*Petroselinum crispum*), rosemary (*Rosmarinus officinalis*), tarragon (*Artemisia dracunculus*), and thyme (*Thymus hirsutis*). Keep them outside during the summer with plenty of sun, water when dry, and give them a sunny window in winter. Don't fertilize these herbs if you want aromatic foliage.

Sword Grass

Every year in late spring garden centers, especially if located near cemeteries, offer a decorative plant arrangement of a few geraniums, a bit of ivy, and a green rosette of swordlike leaves stuck exactly in the center of the pot. The leaves are tapered, about a half inch in width and a foot long. It's difficult to imagine that this "grass" is, in reality, a seedling of *Cordyline australis* that eventually becomes a forty-foot tree in its native New Zealand.

Three years ago, at a July clearance sale, I bought a pot of this imaginative arrangement for ninety-eight cents. The "grass" caught my eye, as the leaves had a leathery and permanent look. I repotted the grass in a five-inch pot, and brought it indoors before frost. That was three years ago. Now the trunk is six inches high and boasts some forty leaves, many two feet in length.

Use the standard potting mix, and repot every two years; don't bother with plant food. Sword grass responds beautifully to root pruning, so if potbound, try this method first. It prefers shade during the early afternoons of summer. Reduce watering during the deep winter months when the plant is dormant. Propagate with seeds from nurseries (it probably will never flower at home) or stem sections.

Wax Begonias

One of the ever-popular bedding plants for summer gardens is the wax begonia (*Begonia semperflorens*). Every year, gardeners buy boxes full of these plants, setting them in partially shaded spots where they bloom all summer and die with the first frost. These begonias are really perennials, and if dug up and potted in the standard mix, will reward you with almost continuous bloom throughout the winter. Initially the plants should be pinched back, removing at least half of each stem to promote bushy growth and new flowers. The cuttings are easily rooted (see Chapter 5) and once started, you will always have plants; start cuttings in April for putting outdoors in window boxes and on sills.

Give these plants full winter sun, water when the soil becomes dry, and keep temperatures on the cool side, usually above 50°F.

- *B. semperflorens* 'Luminosa' has red flowers with light-green waxy leaves that turn to a darker red-brown with strong light in summer.

- *B. semperflorens* 'Pink Pearl' has flowers exactly like its name; the leaves are a light, waxy green.

NOTE: City dwellers, when the Parks Department clears out the summer flower displays, ask for a few of these plants or cuttings.

OTHER GARDEN PLANTS FOR INDOOR BLOOM *

Every fall, as one prepares for endless discussions of chill-factors and degree-days, many flowers of the summer garden continue to bloom, seemingly unaware that the first frost is just about the corner.

The following plants will not bloom all winter, as they eventually perish under home conditions, but if they are potted in August and allowed to remain outdoors until mid-September, their roots will become accustomed to the restraining walls of pots. Given ample sunlight, watering when the soil starts to dry, and temperatures generally below 60°F., they will continue to bloom well into December. Remember also, that nothing ventured, nothing gained; truly a cliché, but an apt statement. Always experiment!

Remember, too, that these plants should be thoroughly checked for insect inhabitants before taken into the home.

- Ageratum (*Ageratum houstonianum*) is a popular bedding plant with bunches of small blue fuzzy flowers.

- Alternanthera is another group of plants with colorful foliage used in elegant plant designs for formal gardens. Grown primarily for leaf color, they make striking accents. If you're lucky, they will hold over till spring, when cuttings can be taken for summer. The two common types are:

- *Alternanthera amoena* has inch-long leaves of red and orange.

- *A. dentata* 'Ruby' has flat, wine-red leaves with purple undersides and is sometimes offered as a house plant.

- Gazania (*Gazania rigens*) is a garden annual that enjoys full sun. The leaves are long and narrow, resting on the ground. Flowers are like

*For a more complete listing of garden and house plants that can be raised from seed at most any time of the year, see the Appendix.

daisies with yellow or orange petals, each marked with a black and white spot at the base. The flowers close at night. In Africa they are perennials and, with luck, these will go through the winter. There are many hybrids of the original gazania.

• Marigolds of the larger varieties are just too big for most homes, and with reduced light become so straggly they are just plain unattractive. But the dwarf marigold (*Tagetes tenuifolia pumila*) never grows above a foot in height. Remove flowers as they fade.

• Nicotiana (*Nicotiana alata grandiflora*) are members of the tobacco family and are prized annuals for the garden. The first time I tried to bring these in, they grew to be six feet tall and produced about three flowers. The next year, I tried the smaller plants and gave them more sun, and the plant flowered until mid-January.

• Petunias (*Petunia* x *hybridida*) are pinched back without mercy, and do very well in a sunny window. They become quite lanky, produce less flowers, but are well worth a try.

• Portulaca (*Portulaca grandiflora*) is a fleshy-leaved garden trailer that closely resembles a common weed, purslane. The flowers are white, red, orange, yellow, or a bright cerise and bloom all summer in the poorest of soils. When lifted from the garden in August, they do amazingly well in pots, continuing to bloom well into December.

• Sweet alyssum (*Lobularia maritima*) will do very well in pots if it is pinched back severely. The flowers are tiny and white.

• Torenia or the wishbone plant (*Torenia fournieri*) is a small perennial generally grown as a garden annual. The plants grow about a foot in height and bear pale-blue flowers, the three lower lobes edged with dark violet and a yellow blotch in the center. Plants can be lifted in the fall or can be sown from seed during August to bloom by early winter. Seeds sown in January bloom in late March.

• Verbena (*Verbena* x *Hybrida*) produces terminal clusters, two to three inches across, of white, pink, yellow, or red flowers that bloom all summer, and indoors well into winter. Cuttings can be taken to provide plants for the following season.

• Violas are the violets and pansies. A European perennial, the Johnny-jump-up (*Viola tricolor*) is now a garden weed in many parts of the northeastern United States, and is the plant that with intense hybridization has produced our modern pansy. The weed seeds freely and continually all summer, so dig up very young plants. With luck, it will bloom for at least a month before getting too leggy. Also try the garden pansy, pinching it back severely before bringing it indoors.

KEEPING GIFT PLANTS ALIVE AND WELL

Every year for Christmas, Valentine's Day, Easter and Mother's Day, the florists of America provide a magnificent display of gift plants for the home. Unfortunately, very few last until the following year.

Instructions follow on caring for azaleas, cyclamen, poinsettia, and, although it's an annual, how to get the most out of calceolaria and grow more.

Azalea

The plants, forced for winter and spring holiday bloom, are evergreen hybrids belonging to the genus *Rhododendron*, but through many years of popular usage are commonly called azaleas.

When receiving an azalea, put it in a cool place with good light; winter sun will shorten flower life, but won't hurt the plant. It will endure a heated room, but should be removed every night to an area not above 65°F. Keep the soil evenly moist and *always* use soft water. Azaleas must have a pH of 4-5. When flowers fade, remove them. If the plant needs repotting, this is the time to do it, using a soil mix of 2 parts peat moss, 1 part potting soil, and 1 part sand.

When all chance of frost is past, place the plant outside for the summer in a sheltered spot; no summer midday sun. Fertilize once a month with an acid fertilizer like Miracid, continuing until fall. Now cut back slightly on water, but never let the soil dry out. Place the plant in a cool location, about 50°F. to set buds. Once the buds have formed, slightly higher temperatures will force flowering, about a year after you received the plant.

Leaves will drop if the soil dries out and leaves will yellow if the soil does not stay on the acid side.

Although it all sounds a bit busy, you'll be rewarded with a magnificent display of flowers.

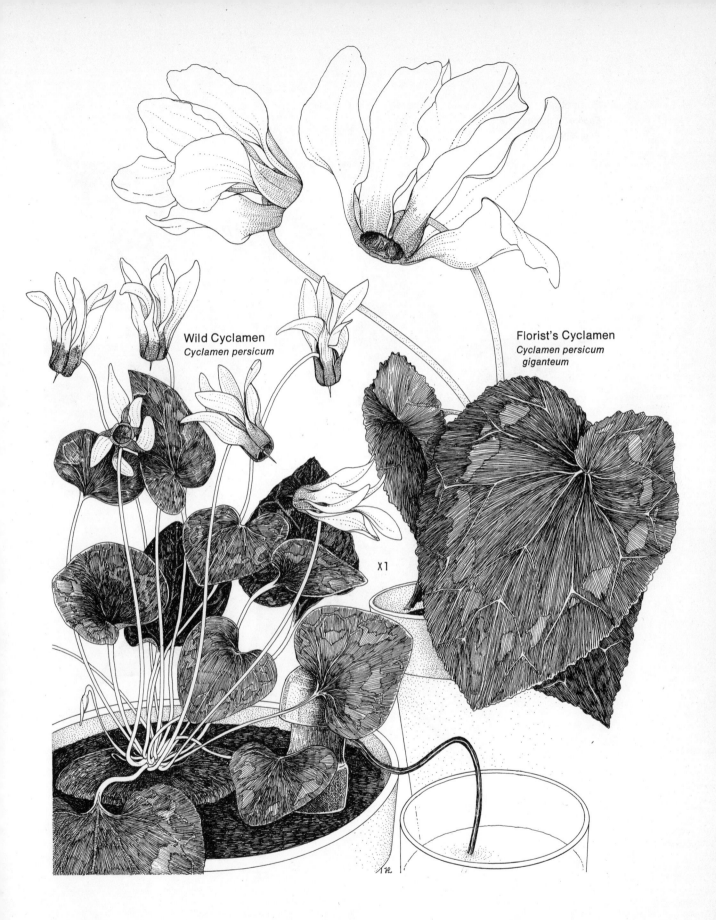

Wild Cyclamen
Cyclamen persicum

Florist's Cyclamen
*Cyclamen persicum
giganteum*

X1

Poinsettia
Euphorbia pulcherrima
'Paul Mikkelsen'

X1

Cyclamen

Of all the flowering plants, this is perhaps my favorite—one reason being that all the advice given on this plant is usually incorrect. Most authorities tell you to dry the tuber after winter bloom and allow it to rest in the summer. The first year I tried that, mice ate the tuber. I then found cultural instructions in an old English garden book, circa 1890, that said to keep the plant in growth all year. I tried this method and the tuber and plant grow larger each year and continually produce more flowers.

If you can't find a cool place for this plant, never buy one or raise it from seed. If it's a gift, enjoy it for the flowers, then give it away. Since the original plant comes from the mountains of Persia where the climate is cool and bright, warm rooms of 65°F. and above shorten flower life and prevent the immature buds from blooming.

The florist's cyclamen (*Cyclamen persicum giganteum*) is available in hybrids of many striking colors with single or double blooms. A large plant may have thirty or more flowers at one time. Add the beautiful patterned leaves, and you have a truly outstanding ornamental plant for most of the year. The illustration depicts a modern hybrid next to the original wild plant, *C. persicum*.

Use the standard soil mix with a pot at least an inch larger that the width of the corm. Soil should never be allowed to dry out or the whole plant will wilt, leaves and flowers quickly bending over the edge of the pot. If this happens, don't despair. Take newspaper and completely surround the pot, starting at one side, slowly putting the stems in an upright position, much like a florist wrapping a bouquet. Fasten the paper and immediately soak the soil. Before the day is out, the stems will absorb enough water to hold themselves up. Don't wait too long for this procedure, or the plant will die back and be forced to provide new leaves. It's a good object lesson: you'll never let it happen again. A self-watering pot, water wicks (you'll need more than one for a large plant) or the Blumat Watering Device pictured with the large cyclamen, are a big help. Never pour water on the crown as the flower buds and tuber should be kept dry to prevent rot. The best time to repot is after the flowers have faded, removing any dead roots at this time.

Give the plant sun in summer, except during midday. In winter, partial shade. During the summer, new leaves will develop before the old leaves wither. During the winter try to keep temperatures about 60°F. During the summer, keep the plant as cool as you can, misting the leaves daily in very hot weather. Fertilize established plants every two weeks in summer and once a month in winter. When removing dead flowers or leaves, give the stems a sharp twist before pulling from the tubers.

If you become interested in cyclamens, they are easy to raise from seed; detailed instructions come with the packet. Or you might branch out and grow the garden varieties which are smaller, more delicate, and some have fragrant blossoms. Follow the same general instructions for the garden forms.

Poinsettia

These Christmas gift plants (*Euphorbia pulcherrima*) are members of a large family of succulents, all having a milky sap called latex. The red "petals" are really bracts, and the small arrows in the illustration point to the real male (♂) and female (♀) flowers. The tips of the flowers produce small drops of nectar. If given proper care, these plants become perennial house plants and can be forced to bloom every year.

Pot in the standard mix and fertilize established plants every two weeks during the summer. Pot plants in May, cutting back the branches to below the bloom.

After the blossoms have faded, prune the stems to below the point of flowering. If the wounds persist in bleeding sap, a quick dip in warm water will congeal the latex. Put the plants outside, if possible, shading from the hot noonday sun, and bring them in before frost. They want full sun in fall and winter to intensify the color of the bracts.

Always keep the soil evenly moist and use lukewarm water. Never allow the soil to dry out or the leaves will drop. If the leaves fall, they'll sprout again but flowering will be delayed. Fertilize established plants once a month in summer.

Repot plants in spring, using the standard mix, removing most of the old soil. Poinsettias are short-day plants. In order to make them set buds and develop the colorful bracts, they must not have more than twelve hours of light out every twenty-four. Even the light from a lamp in an adjoining room will prevent eventual flowering. A practical solution is to put the plant in a

Pocketbook Flower
Calceolaria herbeohybrida

X 3 / 4

closet every night, or cover with a large, opaque sac. For Christmas bloom, start the procedure around the first of October. If your plant room is completely dark after sunset, the process will occur naturally.

Room temperatures are fine for this plant, but the bracts last longer when below 65°F.

A white poinsettia, called *E. pulcherrima* 'Ecke's White' is now available on the market. It is, in many ways, more attractive than the red variety.

Pocketbook Plant

This flower is truly unique in the plant world and you either like it or have a distinct distaste for the whole plant. Dwarf varieties are often used for outdoor bedding plants in cool climates, but its chief *forté* is as a gift plant. Called *Calceolaria herbeohybrida* they are perennials from the mountains of South America, and in our climate treated as annuals since they grow easily from seed. When received as a gift plant, they generally don't do too well because of the same old problem, heat. In a city like New York, early summer forces them into a complete and total collapse, so if you like the plants, the secret is to grow for spring blooming.

Use the standard potting mix, and let the soil dry between waterings. Always keep these plants from the heat of the sun. They prefer shade.

Seeds sewn in September will flower before March and the dwarf varieties will sometimes bloom within three months. Use Jiffy-7's and move to three-inch pots when a few leaves have formed. In about three months they are ready for four-inch pots and flowering.

Discard the plants after flowers fade and start anew in the fall.

Colors are brilliant reds, yellows and oranges, many with darker spots.

FOUR FAVORITE HOUSE PLANTS

Here are four house plants of long standing, two for flowers and two for foliage. None make any great demands on the indoor gardener.

Cast-iron Plant

A Chinese import to Victorian England, the cast-iron plant (*Aspidistra elator*) will tolerate

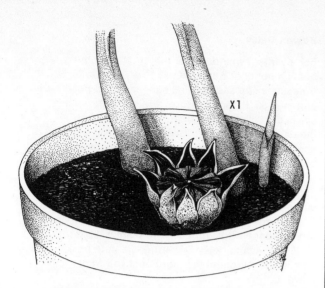

X1

conditions that would kill most other plants, including many weeds. The leaves are a leathery, dark-green, up to two and a half feet long. A large plant takes many years to achieve, but the same effect can be had by potting a number of smaller plants in a six-inch pot. Use the standard mix and repot every two or three years. Keep the soil evenly moist and in a shady spot with temperature averaging 65°F.. If you follow these directions, the plant will grow very well and occasionally small purple flowers will appear at the soil level.

If you forget to water, even for days on end, or move it to a dark corner forgetting the plant entirely for weeks, it will still survive, hence the common name. I'm not suggesting you follow this procedure, but this plant will stand up to neglect.

Jade Plant

Often overlooked at the five and dime because of its small stature, the jade plant (*Crassula argentea*) will surprise you with a beautiful specimen after three or four years of growth. Since it's a succulent, it will stand mistreatment. It prefers sun but will exist in a north window; it won't complain until the leaves begin to shrivel; and though preferring an average temperature of 65°F., it will take summer heat and winter cold to 45°F. When a jade plant gets to be about seven years old, it will flower with clusters of pinkish, starlike blooms.

Pot every other year in the standard mix, give full sun if possible, to bring out the leaf edging of red, and water when the soil is dry.

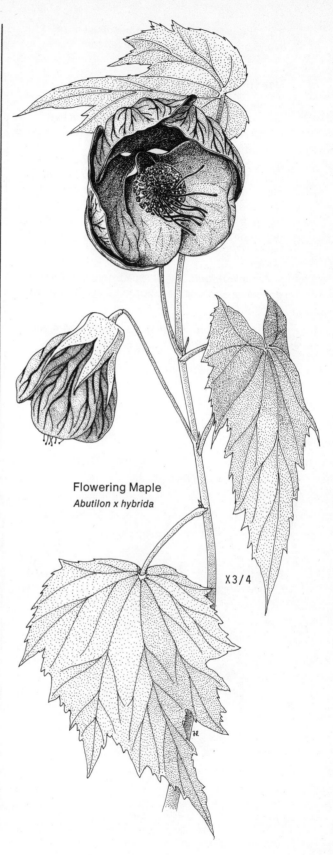

Flowering Maple
Abutilon x hybrida

X3/4

As the jade plant grows, it becomes a tree, eventually reaching a height of ten feet.

Flowering Maple

Another oldtime favorite is the flowering maple (*Abutilon* x *Hybrida*) that produces attractive leaves resembling a maple leaf and lovely, bell-shaped flowers. When given good treatment, the plant develops into a large shrub up to five feet high. Use the standard potting mix, keep evenly moist, and give it full sun all year. It prefers a temperature of 60°F. Flowering maples will bloom a good part of the year, but mainly during the summer months. Pinch the tips for a bushier plant.

• *A.* x *hybridum* 'Souvenir de Bonn' has variegated leaves and salmon-colored blossoms veined with crimson.

• *A.* x *hybridum* 'Goldust' has bright-green leaves flecked with gold and orange flowers.

Boston Daisy

For a winter reminder of summer days, nothing beats a potful of Boston daisy (*Chrysanthemum frutescens chrysaster*). Full sun, standard potting mix, 60°F. temperature, and watering when soil is dry will produce beautiful flowers when the days become short. Boston daisy is another short-day plant, like all mums, and will not set bloom unless exposed to daylight twelve hours or less. If you like experiments, try treating this plant the way florists do, when forcing mums for summer bloom. By restricting light to twelve hours a day two months before bloom is desired (and until the buds appear), the plant will bloom. Or if you wish to delay flowering, just turn on a light in the middle of the night until you want the flowers.

Propagate with cuttings.

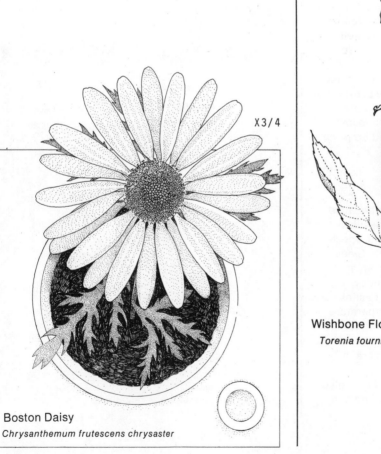

X 3/4

Boston Daisy
Chrysanthemum frutescens chrysaster

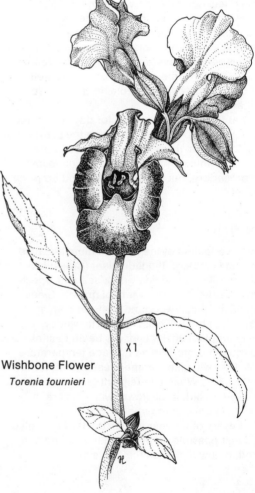

X 1

Wishbone Flower
Torenia fournieri

CHAPTER FIFTEEN
Ailments

Like any living thing, plants are subject to a host of disorders and diseases. I've tried to cover all those ailments that would possibly appear in a home collection of plants. You may be lucky and never have any trouble, or, on the other hand, you may suddenly become convinced that the god of plants is having revenge upon you alone. It's unlikely, unless cursed, that all the symptoms that I describe will show up at any one time, but once you know what to look for, you should be able to treat it.

Many of the symptoms of different problems look the same. Yellowing leaves, for example, can be caused by too little water, or too much heat, or not enough fertilizer. However, if you consider the environmental needs of your plants, and the conditions that you provide, you should be able to sort out the cause of your plant problem. Remember, too, that more than one disorder can exist at the same time. A favored plant might lack humidity yet be overwatered; another might be potbound and short of light at the same time, and then visited by a horde of spider mites. Be very concise and clinical in your approach; list all the unfavorable symptoms that you can see and, with common sense, diagnose a cure.

Symptoms, Causes, and Cures

The following problems are usually associated with watering:

1 When lower leaves wilt, stems become soft, and the soil remains soggy with a green scum forming on the pot, the cause is *too much water.* As a cure, cut back on watering, allowing the soil to dry out between applications; make sure the drain hole is unclogged; don't let plants sit in saucers full of water; and be sure the soil mix has enough material like sand or perlite to guarantee adequate drainage.

2 Leaf edges dry out with the lower leaves turning yellow and falling; brown spots appear on the leaves—the probable cause is *too little water.* To cure, soak the pot completely to saturate the soil. Check the plant's water demands in the cultural notes.

3 The leaf edges turn brown and flakey. This condition is usually caused by *lack of humidity.* Spray plants with a mister, especially on hot days; place the pot on a bed of moist pebbles.

4 Yellow spots appear on leaves, especially those with hairy foliage. Usually caused by *cold water dropped on leaves.* Make sure that all the water you use is at least lukewarm; use a watering can with a spout and go below the leaves.

5 Crown, stem, and leaves become mushy and waterlogged. Generally caused by bacterial rot. When problems develop to this stage, it's best to throw out the plant and, in the future, watch your watering, fertilizing and plant crowding, in that order.

6 Gray scaling appears on the leaves and stems over a long period of time. This is a condition usually caused by *hard water.* If your home water is hard (you can test it with a pH strip) use rainwater or boiled water to prevent calcium build-up. Leaves should be wiped clean.

The following conditions are usually associated with *light*:

1 Leaves toward the light source develop burned areas. This is caused by *sun scorch* and can be remedied by filtering direct sunlight with a screen or light curtain, or by moving the plant to a shadier spot.

2 Leaves curl under and new growth becomes stunted—this is usually symptomatic of *too* *much light.* Shade the plants and check on their individual needs.

3 Stems grow very long and continually lean toward the light source; the new leaves are small. The problem is *too little light.* Move the plant to a stonger light source.

The following conditions are caused by problems of *fertilizing*:

1 Leaves increase in size and amount but the plant produces few or no flowers when it should. Generally caused by *too much fertilizer.* Don't feed the plant for at least a month, and then cut applications by one half.

2 The lower leaves yellow and fall; new leaves are undersized and the stems become stunted. Generally caused by *too little fertilizer.* Increase applications and check on the cultural demands of the plant.

3 A white crust appears on the rim, the sides of the pot and the surface of the soil; stems burn where they touch the deposits. This is caused by a *build-up of fertilizer salts.* Wash the salt off the pot rim; replace the top soil with fresh, and check on the demands of the plant.

4 A green scum forms on pot sides and algal growth starts on the soil. Could be *too much fertilizer.* Decrease applications of plant food by one-half.

The following conditions are caused by a variety of sources.

1 A white fuzz develops on the surface of the stems and leaves. The cause is *mildew.* Isolate the infected plant; wash off the leaves with soap and water, wait a week and wash again. Make sure there is air movement around the plants.

2 Spots of color that have depth appear on the leaves; small growths merge to form larger areas. *A fungus blight.* Cut off the infected parts and isolate the plant. Check air circulation and cut down on humidity. If problem persists, throw the plant out.

3 Leaves suddenly drop off. This is probably caused by *rapid fluctuations in temperature.* Make sure the plants are protected from icy drafts of air. If the condition is rectified the plant will usually produce new leaves.

4 Plant ceases to grow or flower, but is otherwise healthy. Plant has become *dormant.* Cut down on watering and withhold fertilizer until new growth appears.

5 Leaves turn brown, are crushed, bruised, or broken. Continual *brushing by passers-by.* Move the plant to a low-traffic area.

6 Roots crowd the pot and start to grow through the drainage hole. Plant is *potbound.* Repot the plant or trim the roots.

PESTS

You are never aware of the number of disasters, misfortunes, and lethal predators waiting to descend upon the plant world until you become involved in indoor gardening. A tree may harbor beetles, caterpillars, mites, and fungus but remain a thing of beauty; nature provides a wholesome group of predators that strike a balance between destruction and health (unless man enters the scene). However, when plants are brought indoors to a controlled climate, pests can easily follow and *they* are legion. My examples are limited to those I have battled on the home front. There are five common-sense rules that, if followed, go a long way in plant protection. They are:

1 Always quarantine new plants for at least two weeks. Most pests will show up in that time.

2 Keep all plant debris picked up. Don't allow piles of organic litter to accumulate. Litter is a potential breeding ground for trouble.

3 Keep leaves clean and dust-free remembering that dirty leaves cut down on light. Examine the plants while cleaning to spot potential trouble before it gets a stranglehold.

4 No matter how fond you may be of the plant, if the disease is too far gone, destroy both the plant and the soil.

5 Give all plants a thorough inspection after they have summered outside or following the two-week isolation, if they are to join plants in your main collection.

Concerning pesticides, I have an abnormal fear that comes from reading labels. I won't use any except a general house and garden spray (and then with extreme care) and vapona strips. The strips are to be used only in a closed, uninhabited room. You, of course, are free to use any of the scientific pesticide marvels of today, but the following statement by Dr. Henry Cathey, Chief of the Ornamentals Laboratory of the United States Department of Agriculture sums it up for me:

> The major control of houseplant insects is still . . . soapy water, a good scrub brush, and time. You have to do this with some house plants every second day for some time because of the eggs, and it is important to cover the breathing pores of the leaves with soap. This is the alchemy of Grandma's old gardening books. It takes a while but I like to call this "quality time"—time to think, review and relax. Gardeners are returning to it. *

SPIDER MITES

Special honors go to the spider mite for damage above and beyond the call of duty. This ravager of the leaf is found throughout the world and seems to zero in on any plant lover, making its presence known only after near-total calamity. Mites are tiny, but can be seen by a normal pair of eyes as small specks marching up and down the undersurface of a leaf. Once they become established, the female lays about one hundred eggs during a two-week life cycle. Each of these eggs may hatch to produce another hundred, all hungry. The first danger signs are small, white areas that appear on the top of the leaf. Eventually the leaves turn brown and die, but not before they are covered by small webs that generally extend from the leaf edge to the adjoining stem. The webs make control difficult, as they protect the eggs and mites from being dislodged by a strong flow of water, which is the cure usually cited. They like warm, dry conditions; cool and damp surroundings slow them down but don't stop them. Many commercial insecticides are available and mites soon adjust to all of them except the most lethal (both for mite and man). Although it can sometimes be a bit cumbersome, the only safe and effective method I've ever found is soap and water, with weekly applications; once is not enough since you're bound to miss a few eggs.

The first step is to remove the plant from any others, and keep it apart until there is no more evidence of infection. Before scrubbing the plant, cover the soil with a layer of aluminum foil, so the soil will not spill out. A little soap will

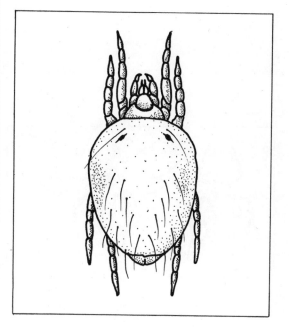

Plants & Gardens; Vol. 29, No. 4, Winter 1973-74. Brooklyn Botanical Garden.

not kill the plant, but practice moderation in all things. (If the plant is too large for the kitchen sink, use the bathtub. If that won't work, take the soap to the plant.) Now, lather up and completely cover both sides of the leaves and the stems with soap. If the leaves are tender use fingers; if leaves are tougher, a small brush will do no harm. After the suds have sat on the leaves for a few minutes, carefully rinse them off. Return the plant to isolation and renew the attack in a week. Perseverance should pay off, but if the plant is beyond help, discard both the plant and the soil.

WHITE FLIES

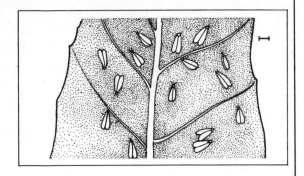

White flies are obnoxious pests that flitter about at the slightest disturbance. The major damage is caused by the larvae which live by sucking the sap from the leaves and in turn excrete a sweet, sticky substance called "honeydew" which becomes a prime target for mold. They breed at a furious rate, and soon form white clouds of annoyance.

If you have a watchful eye, the epidemic can be caught at the start by getting that little white speck that flew at you from the leaf of your favorite morning glory. Having missed it, the next step is a vapona strip. This is the "safe-for-all-homes" impregnated plastic ribbon now sold in most stores. I generally start by removing the plants in the vicinity of the first fly I see to a closed room in company with the vapona. I then keep a watchful eye on the other plants. The strip really works, but only for flying insects.

APHIDS

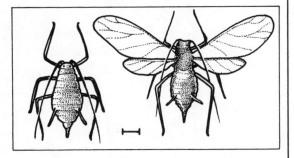

Another group of sap-suckers, aphids are usually brought in from the outdoors. They are slow in movement and possess a complicated and involved life style. They generally overwinter in the soil as eggs that hatch into wingless females which reproduce parthenogenetically in the spring.

After a few generations of more wingless females, they produce winged females that fly on to other plants and produce both males and females that mate and produce eggs for another winter. If found in the spring, you then know they have not spread to other plants. Take the plant and spray with a house-and-garden spray. Be sure to hold the can a good foot from the leaves, since the aerosol propellant is very cold and can freeze plant tissues. Never use unsterilized soil for potting indoors, especially soil from the garden, as it may already harbor aphids.

SCALE

Believe it or not, shellac is made from a scale insect of India. This is the only good thing I've ever heard about this group of insects. The young are too tiny and colorless to be noticed, but are unfortunately quite mobile and walk from stem to leaf. When settled they develop a thick, armored hide and literally glue themselves to the plant and begin to eat. You can flick them off with your fingernail, but another effective means is swabbing them off with a cotton Q-Tip soaked in alcohol.

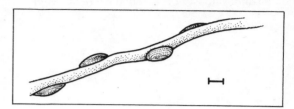

MEALYBUGS

Mealbugs are very common pests, closely related to scale, that resemble small mounds of cotton. Use the Q-Tip and alcohol solution for control. With these and all of the other insects described, remember that they are easily controlled if caught at the beginning. The longer they go unnoticed, the worse they become.

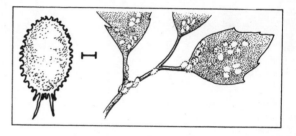

SLUGS

Slugs are shell-less snails, and once you see one, you'll know why shells were invented by nature. The first sign of their presence are glistening silver trails found on the leaves in the early morning, a trail they leave behind as they return to the damp and cold of pot bottoms, escaping the heat of the day. The next sign is the gaping holes they have chewed, and they are capable of doing a great deal of chewing in one night. If you are in an area where slugs are found, make sure all the drainage holes in pots are covered with a small piece of screening.

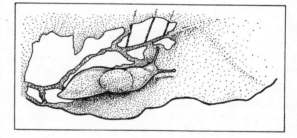

Do your hunting at night, with a flashlight, and pick them off, or if squeamish, drop a small pinch of salt on them, and they'll dissolve like the witch in the *Wizard of Oz*. A tin of beer is said to drown them but I think it just leads to drunken slugs.

ANTS

Aside from carpenter ants that eat foundations, army ants pillaging jungles, fire ants with their painful bite, and red ants that crawl up your pants leg unnoticed, exactly what is wrong with ants in the house? I really cannot say but will continue to rout them out at the first sign of invasion. While not a danger to plants, they have an annoying habit of entering the house after heavy rains or the oncoming winter, where they proceed to nest usually in any pot with an uncovered drainage hole and osmunda or fern fiber. If you see any marching in a straightforward manner, check for their nest and use a house-and-garden spray

issues dealing with specifics of houseplants, indoor light gardening, orchids, ferns, and many other subjects are always in print.

MAGAZINES

Flower and Garden is a bimonthly magazine that often has articles dealing with plants for indoor gardening.
4251 Pennsylvania Avenue
Kansas City, Missouri 64111

Horticulture is a monthly magazine that continually increases its coverage of houseplants.
P. O. Box 53879
Boulder, Colorado 80321

Plants and Gardens is a quarterly published by the Brooklyn Botanical Garden and covers a different garden theme with each issue. The backlist has many excellent issues on indoor gardening and plants that will live in the home.
1000 Washington Avenue
Brooklyn, New York 11225

PLANT SOCIETIES

The following plant societies are dedicated to the pursuit of special interests as their names imply. Memberships usually include special publications, seed exchanges, and invitations to regional meetings. Many groups publish bulletins that are among the most professional in the plant world. *The Bulletin* of the American Orchid Society is as large as T.V. Guide. Find one that interests you and expand your garden horizons.

Actinidia Enthusiasts Newsletter
P. O. Box 1064
Tonasket, WA 98855

African Violet Society
Box 3609
Beaumont, TX 77704

African Violet Society of Canada
8 Smith St.
Moncton, NB E1C 8G2, Canada

American Bamboo Society
1101 San Leon Ct.
Solana Beach, CA 16505

American Begonia Society
Box 1129
Encinitas, CA 92024

American Bonsai Society
Box 385
Keene, New Hampshire 03431

American Boxwood Society
Box 85
Boyce, VA 22620

CHAPTER SIXTEEN
Sources of Supply

Although a few people are fortunate enough to live next door to a commercial greenhouse, most of us must turn to mail-order nurseries when looking for plants and supplies. While most supermarkets today stock a small number of plants and variety stores have plant counters, the choice is usually very limited. So send for catalogues, sit back, relax, and shop by mail.

The best time to order plants is in the spring and fall. Many nurseries will not ship during the hot months of July and August nor in January and February. The suppliers listed here are, to my knowledge, helpful, courteous, and generally efficient. The science of packing plants for United Parcel shipment has been raised to a fine art and is usually quite successful.

If you have any particular interests, it's a good idea to join a plant society as they all publish specialty magazines and newsletters dealing with plant care and cultivation.

The publications of the Brooklyn Botanic Garden are tops in their field. Each year they put out four new and excellent handbooks on a wide range of horticultural subjects, and back

American Bryological and Lichenological Society
Missouri Botanical Garden
2345 Tower Grove Ave.
St. Louis, MO 63110

American Camellia Society
Box 1217
Fort Valley, GA 31030

American Conifer Society
1825 North 72 St.
Philadelphia, PA 19151

American Daffodil Society
2302 Byhalia Rd.
Hernando, MS 38632

American Dahlia Society
159 Pine Street
New Hyde Park, NY 11041

American Fern Society
Botany Dept.
University of Tennessee
Knoxville, TN 37916

American Fuchsia Society
Hall of Flowers
Golden Gate Park
9th Ave. and Lincoln Way
San Francisco, CA 94122

American Ginger Society
P. O. Box 600
Archer, FL 32618

American Gloxinia Society
Box 493
Beverly Farms, MA 01915

American Gourd Society
Box 274
Mount Gilead, OH 43338

American Hemerocallis Society
Route 5, Box 874
Palatka, FL 32077

American Hibiscus Society
Drawer 5430
Pompano Beach, FL 33064

American Hosta Society
9448 Mayfield Road
Chesterland, OH 44026

American Iris Society
Box 10003
Huntsville, AL 35801

American Ivy Society
Box 520
West Carrollton, OH 45449

American Magnolia Society
Box 129
Nanuet, NY 10954

American Orchid Society
6000 South Olive Ave.
West Palm Beach, FL 33405

American Penstemon Society
Box 33
Plymouth, VT 05056

American Peony Society
250 Interlachen Rd.
Hopkins, MN 55343

American Plant Life Society
Box 150
La Jolla, CA 92038
(Amarylis Society)

American Poinsettia Society
Box 706
Mission, TX 78572

American Pomological Society
103 Tyson Bldg.
University Park, PA 16802

American Primrose Society
6730 West Mercer Way
Mercer Island, WA 98040

American Rhododendron Society
14635 S.W. Bull Mountain Rd.
Tigard, OR 97223

American Rose Society
Box 30,000
Shreveport, LA 71130

Aril Society International
5500 Constitution, N.E.
Albuquerque, NM 87110

Azalea Society of America
Box 6244
Silver Spring, MD 20906

Bonsai Canada
12 Beardmore Crescent
Toronto, ON M2K 2P5, Canada

Bonsai Clubs International
Box 2098
Sunnyvale, CA 94087

British Columbia Fuchsia and Begonia Society
2175 West 16th Ave.
Vancouver, BC V6K 3B1, Canada

Bromeliad Society
P. O. Box 41261
Los Angeles, CA 90041

Cactus and Succulent Society of America
2631 Fairgreen Ave.
Arcadia, CA 91006

California Rare Fruit Growers
Fullerton Arboretum, CSU
Fullerton, CA 92634

Canadian Chrysanthemum and Dahlia Society
83 Aramaman Dr.
Agincourt, ON M1T 2P7, Canada

Canadian Geranium and Pelargonium Society
254 West Kings Rd.
North Vancouver, BC V7N 2L9

Canadian Gladiolus Society
1274-129A Street
Surrey, BC V4A 3Y4, Canada

Canadian Iris Society
199 Florence Avenue
Willowdale, ON M2N IG5, Canada

Canadian Rose Society
18-12 Castlegrove Boulevard
Don Mills, ON M3A 1K8, Canada

Carnivorous Plant Society
The Fullerton Arboretum
California State University
Fullerton, CA 92634

Cycad Society
1191 4th Avenue West
Seattle, WA 98119

Cymbidium Society of America
469 W. Norman Ave.
Arcadia, CA 91006

Delphinium Society
1630 Midwest Plaza Bldg.
Minneapolis, MN 55402

Desert Plant Society of Vancouver
2941 Parket St.
Vancouver, BC V5K 2T9, Canada

Dwarf Conifer Notes
Theophrastus, P. O. Box 458
Little Compton, RI 02837

Dwarf Fruit Tree Association
303 Horticulture MSU
East Lansing, MI 48823

Epiphyllum Society of America
Box 1395
Monrovia, CA 91016

Friends of the Fig
840 Ralph Road
Conyers, GA 30208

Gardenia Society of America
Box 879
Atwater, CA 95301

Heliconia Society International
6450 S.W. 81 Street
Miami, FL 33143

Herb Society of America
300 Massachusetts Ave.
Boston, MA 02115

Holly Society of America
304 Northwind Dr.
Baltimore, MD 21204

Home Orchid Society
2511 S.W. Miles St.
Portland, OR 97219

Hoya International
Box 54271
Atlanta, GA 30308

Indoor Citrus and Rare Fruit Society
176 Coronado Avenue
Los Altos, CA 94022

Indoor Gardening Society of America
128 West 58th Street
New York, NY 10019

Indoor Light Gardening Society of America
RD 5, Box 76
East Stroudsburg, PA 18301

International Aroid Society
P. O. Box 43-1853
Miami, FL 33143

International Asclepiad Society
10 Moorside Terrace
Drighlington, BD11 1HX, England

International Cactus and Succulent Society
P. O. Box 253
Odessa, TX 79760

International Clematis Society
Burford House, Tenbury Wells
Worcester, WR15 8HQ, England

International Geranium Society
5861 Walnut Dr.
Eureka, CA 95501

International Lilac Society
Box 315
Rumford, ME 04276

International Palm Society
Box 27
Forestville, CA 95436

International Tropical Fern Society
8720 S.W. 34th St.
Miami, FL 33165

Los Angeles International Fern Society
14895 Gardenhill Dr.
La Miranda, CA 90638

Marigold Society of America
Box 112
New Britain, PA 18901

Men's Garden Clubs of America
5560 Merle Hay Road
Des Moines, IA 50323

National Chrysanthemum Society
2612 Beverly Rd.
Roanoke, VA 24015

National Fuchsia Society
2892 Crown View Drive
Rancho Palos Verdes, CA 90274

National Oleander Society
Box 3431
Galveston Island, TX 77552

Nerine Society
Brookend House
Welland, Worcestershire, England

North American Fruit Explorers
10 S. 055 Madison
Hinsdale, IL 60521

North American Gladiolus Council
8524 Vollmert Ave.
Baltimore, MD 21236

North American Heather Society
62 Elma-Monte Rd.
Elma, WA 98541

North American Lily Society
Box 476
Waukee, IA 50263

Northern Nut Growers Association
Broken Arrow Rd.
Hamden, CT 06518

Palm Society
Box 368
Lawrence, KS 66044

Peperomia Society
100 Neil Ave.
New Orleans, LA 70114

Perennial Plant Association
217 Howlett Hall
2001 Fyffe Court
Columbus, OH 43210

Plumeria Society of America
1014 Riverglyn
Houston, TX 77063

Rare Fruit Council International
13609 Old Cutler Road
Miami, FL 33158

Rhododendron Society of Canada
4271 Lakeshore Road
Burlington, ON L7L 1A7, Canada

Saintpaulia International/Gesneriad Society International
Box 549
Knoxville, TN 37901

Sempervivum Fanciers Association
37 Ox Bow Lane
Randolph, MA 02368

Society of Louisiana Irises
Box 40175 USL
Lafayette, LA 70504

Soil Conservation Society of America
7515 Ankeny Road
Ankeny, IA 50021

Solana Newsletter
3370 Princeton Ct.
Santa Clara, CA 95051

Terrarium Association
54 Wolfpit Ave.
Norwalk, CT 06851

Toronto Gesneriad Society
70 Enfield Rd.
Etobicoke, ON M8W 1T9, Canada

Vancouver Island Rock and Alpine Society
575 Towner Road, RR1
Sidney, BC V82 3R9, Canada

Waterlily Society of America
Box 104
Lilypons, MD 21717

Wildflowers
35 Bauer Crescent
Unionville, Ontario I3R 4H3, Canada

SOURCES OF SUPPLY

Plants and Seeds:

Altman Specialty Plants
553 Buena Creek Road
San Marcos, California 92069
Unusual succulents from around the world.

The Banana Tree
715 Northampton Street
Easton, Pennsylvania 18042
Seeds for bananas, trees, and flowers.

BioQuest International
P. O. Box 5752
Santa Barbara, CA 93150
Many interesting South African seeds and bulbs.

Chiltern Seeds
Bortree Stile,
Ulverston, Cumbria LA12 7PB, England
One of the largest collections of seeds in the world.

The Country Garden
Route 2, Box 455A
Crivitz, Wisconsin 54114
Large collection of seeds.

Endangered Species
12571 Red Hill Avenue
Tustin, California 92680
Bamboos and many unusual indoor and outdoor plants.

Glasshouse Works
Church Street, Box 97
Stewart, Ohio 45778
Traditional and unusual plants.

Greenlife Gardens Greenhouses
101 County Line Road
Griffin, Georgia 30223
Huge selection of epiphyllums.

Hortica Gardens
P. O. Box 308
Placerville, California 95667
Many plants for bonsai training.

C. W. Hosking
P. O. Box 500, Hayle
Cornwall, England
Tropical seeds both rare and unusual.

J. L. Hudson, Seedsman
P. O. Box 1058
Redwood City, California 94064
A huge selection of seeds from all over the world.

International Growers Exchange
P. O. Box 52248
Livonia, Michigan 48152
A clearing house for unusual plants.

Logee's Greenhouses
Danielson, Connecticut 06239
A vast collection of indoor plants.

Maver Rare Perennials
Route 2, Box 265B
Asheville, North Carolina 28805
Seeds from around the world.

McClure & Zimmerman
1422 West Thorndale
Chicago, Illinois 60660
Many unusual bulbs.

Geo. W. Park Seed Company
Greenwood, South Carolina 29647
Large selection of unusual seeds.

Peter Paul's Nurseries
Canandaigua, New York 14424
Complete selection of insectivores.

Sandy Mush Herbs
Route 2, Surrett Cove Road

Leicester, North Carolina 28748
Diverse selection of herbs.

Stallings Nursery
910 Encinitas Boulevard
Encinitas, California 92024
Exotic flowering plants.

Thompson & Morgan
P. O. Box 100
Farmingdale, New Jersey
One of England's oldest seed houses with a vast selection of seeds.

Thompson's Begonias
P. O. Drawer PP
Southampton, New York 11968
World's most complete listing of begonias.

We-Du Nurseries
Route 5, Box 724
Marion, North Carolina 28752
A large collection of native wildflowers.

Woodlanders
1128 Colleton Avenue
Aiken, South Carolina 29801
Many fine wildflowers and plants.

Supplies and Equipment

Charley's Greenhouse Supplies
P. O. Box 2110
LaConner, Washington 98257

Mellinger's
2310 W. South Range Road
North Lima, Ohio 44452

Walt Nicke
Box 433 H, McLeod Land
Topsfield, Massachusetts 01983
The original garden supermarket.

NEW, OLD AND RARE BOOKS DEALING WITH HORTICULTURE AND BOTANY

The American Botanist
P. O. Box 143
Brookfield, Illinois 60513
Herbals, horticulture, and garden history.

Warren F. Broderick
695 4th Avenue
P. O. Box 124
Lansingburgh, New York 12182
Books new and old.

Capability's Books
Box 114 Highway 46
Deer Park, Wisconsin 54007
All the newest books.

Elisabeth Woodburn
Booknoll Farm
Hopewell, New Jersey 08525
Many unusual books.

Appendix

APPENDIX A

**A PARTIAL LISTING
OF PLANTS GROWN FROM SEED
SOWN AT ANY TIME OF THE YEAR:**

B = *flowers*   F = *foliage*

Achimenes spp.   (B)
African violet (*Saintpaulia*) spp.   (B)
Amaryllis (*Hippeastrum*) spp.   (B)
Amazon lily (*Eucharis grandiflora*)   (B)
Aralia (*Dizygotheca elegantissima*)   (F)
Asparagus fern (*Asparagus*) spp.   (F)

Balsam (*Impatiens balsamina*)   (B)
Begonia (*Begonia*) spp.   (B)
Bird-of-paradise (*Strelitzia reginae*)   (B)
Bougainvillea spp.   (B)
Browallia spp.   (B)
Butterfly pea (*Clitoria ternatea*)   (B,F)

Cactus, most species   (B,F)
Cardinal climber (*Quamoclit sloteri*)   (B,F)
Clivia spp.   (B,F)
Cobra lily (*Darlingtonia californica*)   (F)
Coleus spp.   (F)
Coral vine (*Antigonon leptopus*)   (B,F)
Cordyline spp.   (F)
Cypress vine (*Quamoclit pennata*)   (B,F)

Echeveria spp.   (B,F)
Exacum spp.   (B)

Ferns, most species   (F)
Flag of Spain (*Quamoclit lobata*)   (B,F)
Flame violet (*Episcia*) spp.   (B,F)
Flowering maple (*Abutilon*) spp.   (B,F)
Freesia x hybrida   (B)
Fuchsia spp.   (B)
Firecracker plant (*Gesneria cuneifolia*)   (B)

Gloriosa lily (*Gloriosa*) spp.   (B)
Glory pea (*Clianthus formosus*)   (B,F)
Gloxinia (*Sinningia*) spp.   (B)

Heliotrope spp.   (B)
Hoya spp.   (B,F)

Ice plant (*Mesembryanthemum crystallinum*)
   (B,F)
Impatiens spp.   (B)

Jacaranda mimosifolia   (B,F)
Jasmine (*Jasminum*) spp.   (B,F)

Kalanchoe spp.   (B,F)
Kudzu vine (*Pueraria thunbergiana*)   (F)

Lantana spp.   (B)
Lily-of-the-Nile (*Agapanthus africanus*)   (B,F)
Living stones, (*Lithops*) spp.   (B,F)

Mandevilla suaveolens   (B,F)
Marguerite (*Felicia bergeriana*)   (B)
Marble vine (*Bryonopsis laciniosa*)   (B,F)
Mimosa (*Acacia*) spp.   (B,F)
Monkey flower (*Mimulus aurantiacus*)   (B)
Morning glories (*Ipomoea*) spp.   (B,F)
Montbretia (*Tritonia)* spp.   (B)

Nasturtium (*Tropaeolum*) spp.   (B,F)

Oleander (*Nerium oleander*)   (B,F)
Orange (*Citrus*) spp.   (B,F)
Ornithogalum spp.   (B)
Oxalis spp.   (B,F)

Palms, most species   (F)
Passion flower (*Passiflora*) spp.   (B,F)
Pentas lanceolata   (B)
Peperomia spp.   (B,F)
Peppers (*Capsicum*) spp.   (B,F)
Philodendron spp.,   (F)
Pineapple lily (*Eucomis zambesiaca*)   (B)
Plumbago capensis   (B,F)
Pocketbook plant (*Calceolaria*) spp.   (B)
Poinciana pulcherrima   (B)
Polka dot plant, (*Hypoestes sanguinolenta*) (F)
Punica spp.   (B,F)

Rhoicissus spp.   (F)

Schizanthus spp.   (B)
Sedum, most species   (B,F)
Sempervivum, most species   (B,F)
Silk oak (*Grevillea*) spp.   (B,F)
Sprekelia formosissima   (B)

Streptocarpus spp.   (B,F)

Torenia fournieri   (B)
Transvaal daisy (*Gerbera jamesonii*)   (B)

Venus flytrap (*Dionaea muscipula*)   (F)

Zephyranthes grandifolia   (B)

APPENDIX B

CHART OF pH VALUES
FOR COMMON PLANTS

(*see graph on page 29*)

African violet (*Saintpaulia*) spp.   (B)
Ageratum houstonianum   (B)
Alyssum (*Lobularia*) spp.   (B)
Amaryllis (*Hippeastrum*) spp.   (C)
Asparagus spp.   (B)
Avocado *Persea americana*)   (B)

Banana (*Musa nana*)   (B)
Begonia spp.   (C)
Bleeding heart (*Dicentra spectabilis*)   (B)
Bloodroot (*Sanguinaria canadensis*)   (C)

Citrus spp.   (C)

Clematis spp.   (A)
Coffee plant (*Coffea arabica*)   (D)
Coleus spp.   (B)
Columbine (*Aquilegia canadensis*)   (B)
Crocus spp.   (B)
Cyclamen spp.   (C)

Ferns, most spp.   (D)
Fuchsia spp.   (B)

Gardenia spp.   (C)
Geranium (*Pelargonium*) spp.   (A)

Heliotrope spp.   (A)
Hepatica noblis   (B)
Hyacinth spp.   (B)
Hydrangea spp. Blue flowers   (E)
         ''   Pink   ''   (C)

Jack-in-the-pulpit (*Arisaema triphyllum*)   (D)

Ladyslipper, yellow, (*Cypripedium calceolus*)   (B)
Ladyslipper, pink, (*C. acaule*)   (E)
Lilium spp.   (C)
Lobelia spp.   (B)

Mimosa (*Acacia*) spp.   (A)
Morning glories (*Ipomoea*) spp.   (A)

Nasturtium (*Tropaeolum*) spp.   (A)

Oxalis spp.   (B)

Petunia x hybrida   (A)
Passion flower (*Passiflora*) spp.   (B)
Pineapple (*Ananas comosus*)   (C)
Pitcher plant (*Sarracenia*) spp.   (B)
Poinsettia (*Euphorbia*) spp.   (B)
Pot marigold (*Calendula officinalis*)   (B)

Sweet potato (*Ipomoea batatas*)   (C)
Star of Bethlehem (*Ornithogalium*) spp.   (B)

Transvaal daisy (*Gerbera jamesonii*)   (B)
Trailing arbutus (*Epigaea repens*)   (E)
Trillium spp.   (B)

Venus flytrap (*Dionaea muscipula*)   (E)

APPENDIX C

MEASURING FOOT CANDLES WITH AN IN-A-CAMERA REFLECTED LIGHT METER

Set film speed to ASA 200 and shutter speed at 1/500 second

F22	5000 FC	F 8	550 FC
F16	2500 FC	F 6.3	300 FC
F11	1200 FC	F 4.5	150 FC

APPENDIX D

MEASURING FOOT CANDLES WITH A WESTON-TYPE METER

Reading	Foot Candles	Reading	Foot Candles
2	.4	10	100.
3	.8	11	200.
4	1.6	12	400.
5	3.2	13	800.
6	6.4	14	1600.
7	12.8	15	3200.
8	26.	16	6400.
9	52.		

Bibliography

Baines, J., and Key, Katherine
The ABC of Indoor Plants
New York: Alfred A. Knopf, 1973

Ballard, Ernesta Drinker
Garden In Your House
New York: Harper & Row, 1971

Britton, N. L., and Rose, J. N.
The Cactaceae. 4 vols. 1937
Reprint (4 vols. in 2)
New York: Dover Publications, 1963

Bruggeman, L.
Tropical Plants
London: Thames and Hudson, 1962

Cobb, Boughton
A Field Guide to the Ferns
Boston: Houghton Mifflin Company, 1956

Crockett, James Underwood
Greenhouse Gardening as a Hobby
New York: Doubleday & Company, Inc., 1961

Elbert, George A.
The Indoor Light Gardening Book
New York: Crown Publishers, Inc., 1973

Fink, Bruce
The Lichen Flora of The United States
Ann Arbor: The University of Michigan Press, 1961

Flawn, L. N. and V. L.
The Cool Greenhouse All The Year Round
London: John Gifford Limited, 1966

Foster, F. Gordon
Ferns To Know And Grow
New York: Hawthorn Books, Inc., 1971

Genders, Roy
Bulbs, A Complete Handbook
New York: Bobbs-Merrill Company, Inc., 1973

Graf, Alfred Byrd
Exotica 6
New Jersey: Roehr's Company, 1973

Graf, Alfred Byrd
Exotic Plant Manual
New Jersey: Roehr's Company, 1970

Grout, A. J.
Mosses With Handlens and Microscope
1903. Reprint.
Ashton, Maryland: Eric Lundberg, 1965

Hale, Mason E., Jr.
Lichen Handbook
Washington: Smithsonian Institution Press, 1968

Healey, B. J.
A Gardener's Guide to Plant Names
New York: Charles Scribner's Sons, 1972

Krauss, Helen K.
Begonias for American Homes and Gardens
New York: The Macmillan Company, 1947

Lamb, Edgar and Brian
The Pocket Encyclopedia of Cacti and Succulents
New York: The Macmillan Company, 1970

Lloyd, Francis Ernest
The Carnivorous Plants
Waltham, Massachusetts:
Chronica Botanica Company, 1942

Muller, Walter H.
Botany, A Functional Approach
New York: The Macmillan Company, 1974

Nicolaisen, Age
The Pocket Encyclopedia of Indoor Plants
New York: The Macmillan Company, 1970

Northern, Rebecca Tyson
Home Orchid Growing
New York: Van Nostrand Reinhold Company, 1970

Padilla, Victoria
Bromeliads
New York: Crown Publishers, Inc. 1973

Parsons, Frances Theodora
How To Know The Ferns
New York: Charles Scribner's Sons, 1927

Peterson, Roger Tory, and McKenny, Margaret
A Field Guide to Wildflowers
Boston: Houghton Mifflin Company, 1968

Richter, Walter
Orchid Care
New York: The Macmillan Company, 1972

Rickett, Harold William
*Wildflowers of The United States:
The North-Eastern States*. Vol. 1
New York: McGraw-Hill Book Company, 1967

Rickett, Harold William
*Wildflowers of The United States:
The South-Eastern States*. Vol. 2
New York: McGraw-Hill Book Company, 1967

Round, F. E.
Introduction to The Lower Plants

New York: The Plenum Press, 1969

Simmons, Alan E.
Growing Unusual Fruit
New York: Walker and Company, 1972

Synge, Patrick M.
The Complete Guide to Bulbs
New York: E. P. Dutton and Company, Inc., 1962

Torrey, John G.
Development in Flowering Plants
New York: The Macmillan Company, 1967

Wilson, Robert Gardner and Catherine
Bromeliads in Cultivation
Coconut Grove, Florida:
Hurricane House Publishers, Inc., 1964

Index

Torenia, 138
    fournieri, 138, 144
Tradescantia
    blossfoldiana, 82
    sillamontana, 82
Transpiration, 3
Transplantation of roots, 8
Trillium
    erectum, 111
    grandiflorum, 111
    luteum, 111
    undulatum, 111
Tropical ferns, 52
Tuber nasturtium, 66
Tubers, 9
Tulip, 12, 29, 128
    Red Emperor, 131
    terminal bud, 5
Tulipa fosteriana, 128, 131

U

Umbel (onion family), 12

V

Venus flytrap plant, 124, 125
Verbena, 138
Verbena X *hybrida*, 138
Vines, about the window, 57-68
Viola tricolor, 138
Violas, 138
Virginia creeper, 10

W

Wandering Jew, 81, 82
    bronze, 81
    tricolor, 81

Water
    application with an atomizer, 3
    for cytoplasm, 4
    for photosynthesis process, 4
    hydrogen in, 2
    in life of a cell, 2
    loss of, 4
    vapor, 2
Watsonia, 133
Watsonia humilis maculata, 133
Wax begonias, 137
Weeds, grassy, 9
White flies, 148
Wild cyclamen, 139
Wild flowers, 5, 109-116
Wild ginger, 113
Wintergreen, 115
Wishbone flower, 144

Z

Zebrina
    pendula, 81
    purpusli, 81
Zinnia, 29

Notes

Notes

Notes